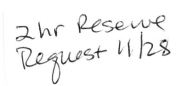

2 hr Reserve
Request 11/28

"We are living through a time when it has become clear to all that business as usual is not an option. Adam Werbach has been on to this for some time—and *Strategy for Sustainability* gives us essential insights that will help us reconstruct an economy that truly enables us to thrive."

—Aron Cramer, CEO,
Business for Social Responsibility

"Werbach's thoughtful approach provides a useful perspective to companies looking to reimagine their opportunities. Business has the opportunity to make real, sustainable change, and this book will help chart the course."

—Kindley Walsh-Lawlor, Senior Director,
Global Responsibility and Environmental Affairs, Gap Inc.

"*Strategy for Sustainability* is a must-read guide for executives looking to craft a coherent strategy after the green bubble. Its real-world case studies on sustainability successes and failures are crucial for anyone who wants to find out how to go beyond green to true sustainability in corporate America."

—Ted Nordhaus and Michael Shellenberger, coauthors of
"The Death of Environmentalism" and *Break Through*

"Soon every company will have a strategy for sustainability. The other option? Extinction. *Strategy for Sustainability* takes Werbach's work with companies like Walmart to a new level."

—Hunter Lovins, author, *Natural Capitalism*

"Adam has bridged the divide between advocates focused on 'sustainability' and business leaders focused on shareholders, accomplishing something that nonprofits and socially responsible investment funds have long endeavored to do. This is a great book!"

—Jigar Shah, CEO, SunEdison

"It's pretty clear by now that standard operating procedure for our businesses works badly both for the bottom line and the planet. New ideas are needed, and Adam Werbach has rustled up a bunch of them—I don't agree with every example in this book, but I find them an intriguing and useful place to start a conversation."

—Bill McKibben, author, *Deep Economy*

"This book is packed with wisdom and inspiration, and provides practical insights and lessons for all types of companies. Adam understands both business and human nature, and this powerful combination allows him to reveal the value of moving beyond compliance to true sustainability."

—Harriet Hentges, VP,
Corporate Responsibility and Sustainability, Ahold USA

"*Strategy for Sustainability* will help define a new era of capitalism—one that addresses the social, economic, environmental, and cultural challenges facing our world today. Using his deep knowledge of environmental issues and his experience as an advocate, Adam presents a compelling argument that should inspire all executives to hold their corporations accountable to a higher standard for sustainability."

—Liz Maw, Executive Director, Net Impact

"*Strategy for Sustainability* provides a game plan that anyone—*Fortune* 500 CEO, small-business owner, or serial entrepreneur—can follow to help their business win for the long term."

—Andrew Beebe, Managing Director,
Suntech Energy Solutions

"Business as usual won't work anymore—for business, or society. The planet can't support it, and the people won't allow it. Fortunately, Werbach has written a step-by-step guide for companies that want to reorient and thrive. CEOs, read this book!"

—Justin Ruben, Executive Director, MoveOn.org

"Just like the people of New Orleans so eloquently portrayed in the opening pages of Adam Werbach's manifesto, people in my own South Bronx and places like it everywhere have been the victims of the same shortsighted 'planning.' *Strategy for Sustainability* gives me hope that decision makers at all levels will look ahead before they act, and make choices we can all be proud of. Thank you Adam!"

—Majora Carter, urban revitalization strategist

"In the venture capital community, we're seeing companies leverage a strategy for sustainability to create a core competitive advantage in the marketplace."

—Josh Becker, Founder and General Partner,
New Cycle Capital

STRATEGY FOR SUSTAINABILITY

STRATEGY FOR SUSTAINABILITY

A BUSINESS MANIFESTO ADAM WERBACH

HARVARD BUSINESS PRESS BOSTON, MASSACHUSETTS

No part of this publication may be reproduced, stored in or introduced into a retrieval system, or transmitted, in any form, or by any means (electronic, mechanical, photocopying, recording, or otherwise), without the prior permission of the publisher. Requests for permission should be directed to permissions@hbsp.harvard.edu, or mailed to Permissions, Harvard Business School Publishing, 60 Harvard Way, Boston, Massachusetts 02163.

Library of Congress Cataloging-in-Publication Data

Werbach, Adam.
  Strategy for sustainability: a business manifesto / Adam Werbach.
    p. cm.
   ISBN 978-1-4221-7770-9 (hardcover : alk. paper) 1.   Strategic planning.
2.   Sustainable development. I.   Title.
  HD30.28.W388 2009
  658.4'012—dc22

                        2009000802

The paper used in this publication meets the requirements of the American National Standard for Permanence of Paper for Publications and Documents in Libraries and Archives Z39.48-1992.

This book is printed on paper certified by the Forest Stewardship Council (FSC) The FSC is an independent, non-governmental, not-for-profit organization established to promote the responsible management of the world's forests.

Mixed Sources
Product group from well-managed forests, controlled sources and recycled wood or fiber
www.fsc.org   Cert no. SGS-COC-005368
© 1996 Forest Stewardship Council

To my love Lyn

and our children

Mila, Pearl, and Sy

Nature's Rules of Sustainability

Diversify across generations.

Adapt and specialize to the changing environment.

Celebrate transparency.

Plan and execute systemically, not compartmentally.

Form groups and protect the young.

Integrate metrics.

Improve with each cycle.

Rightsize regularly, rather than downsize occasionally.

Foster longevity, not immediate gratification.

Waste nothing, recycle everything, and borrow little.

Contents

What Do We Mean by "Strategy for Sustainability"?

I N 1997, I went to New Orleans to meet with the mayor about the city's preparations for the effects of climate change. My role as an environmentalist was to enlist governments in effecting the changes I wanted to see in the world: specifically, I wanted the U.S. Army Corps of Engineers to speed up its wetlands restoration projects near the Mississippi.

Wetlands are nature's sponges. If you take away the wetlands, then you take away an ecosystem's capacity to cope with the extra water from a storm. Anyone who studied the situation understood how critical the wetlands were to New Orleans' survival; we had to protect them. I was advocating a plan that would rebuild the city's levees and restore the wetlands simultaneously.

As I landed in New Orleans, I saw smoke. The city's water treatment plant was on fire. I rushed straight to the mayor's ornate and spacious office, expecting him to shorten our meeting because of the fire. But there he was, unconcerned about the fire. He greeted me jokingly, "That type of stuff happens all the time here."

I made my pitch. Imagine your kitchen table full of dish sponges. Now pour a glass of water on the table. The sponges soak up all the water, so that nothing spills to the floor. Next, take away half the sponges. That is what the United States has done in the last two hundred years; it has destroyed half the country's wetlands.[1] Now imagine that, thanks to the trends in climate change, the glass of water grows into a pitcher of water, since increasingly warmer climate increases the frequency and severity of storms like the ones that cycle through the Gulf of Mexico. When you pour the pitcher's contents on the table, water floods onto the floor. Wetlands play an essential ecological service, and when they've been destroyed, it's only a matter of time before disaster strikes.

I explained the science, showed the maps of the threats to New Orleans, and presented the funding proposal that I wanted him to support. He smiled and told me his staff would follow up with me shortly. Then he gave me a ceremonial key to the city, thanked me for my passionate advocacy, and showed me the door. I never heard back from him or his office. I tried to rally support a few more times there, but only a small group of people cared enough to understand what was at stake, and I couldn't expand that circle.

The key—a golden key stamped with the symbol of the great city of New Orleans—was a heavy reminder of my own failure at communicating the risk and the opportunity. So I gave it to a friend who grew up in New Orleans and who knew better than I what could happen to the city.

Then Katrina hit. She was a category 5 hurricane supercharged by the heated water off the Gulf of Mexico. The levee system failed catastrophically, and the wetlands couldn't keep up with the storm. It was September 2005.

Something breaks inside you when your own failures take on category 5 proportions. My job, what I was paid to do, was to sound alarms *and* to mobilize resources. I had failed. As I watched people stranded on their roofs, bodies floating in the water, I knew we environmentalists could no longer do what we had been doing. Focusing solely on saving the environment did not suffice—did not save lives, livelihoods, or neighborhoods. We needed to fight for a larger kind of sustainability: one that took into account our social, economic, and cultural sustainability as well as our ecological surroundings. I could not be just an environmentalist. I had to think more comprehensively. That was the first big idea I took away from my mistakes and the Katrina disaster.

As I kept watching the news, I noticed that supplies from Walmart seemed to reach the victims faster than the federal government's aid. Then the second big idea hit me: the corporate sector has the incentives, operational know-how, scalability, and ingenuity to respond to the global challenges we face today, challenges on all four fronts—social, economic, environmental, and cultural. Why? Because, by the beginning of the twenty-first century, over half of the world's hundred largest economies were corporations.[2] Walmart's sales in 2007 were greater than the economies of 144 countries, according to the International Monetary Fund.[3] Two-thirds of global trade is accounted for by just five hundred corporations.[4] With this power comes higher expectations. Society increasingly holds global businesses accountable as the only institutions powerful enough to respond at the scale of the challenges that our planet faces. There is no multinational government, but there are many cross-border corporations that witness how resource constraints affect markets, customers, communities, and natural habitats. And this situation gives companies a special opportunity to lead. Business leaders must respond if they hope to maintain their markets and society's license to grow. The crash of an affordable national health system is a burden to citizens and employers. A spike in commodity prices because of resource scarcity is a hardship for producers and consumers. A community that's unable to provide basic foods and comforts for itself won't be a community for long. The turbulence of our modern world makes it more than a corporate responsibility to take into account these external factors. It's a necessity for corporate survival.

This means that corporate and community leaders must also look at the long-term social and cultural consequences of their actions—and their inaction. Because of its short-term focus, the corporate sector—especially energy, real estate, and insurance companies—lost billions of dollars when Katrina hit. Just as I had failed as an environmentalist, these companies had failed as economic fiduciaries to see the knowable future and protect themselves from it. They, too, needed to think more comprehensively.

Above all, Katrina was a human tragedy. Beyond the pelting of the winds, the rains, the waves, it was humans who failed other humans. A strategy that focused narrowly on the environment or the economy or even both would not have prevented the hurricane. What I had failed to lay out for the mayor of New Orleans were the social and the political consequences; the number of voters who would lose their homes and their jobs; the tax consequence of the number of local businesses that would go under; and the number of schools, churches, hospitals, and other community institutions that would close, rendering the whole city unlivable. The energy, real estate, and insurance sectors failed to build their businesses to last in a world in which all these factors—social and cultural among them—were taken into account.

Every business needs these kinds of considerations at the core of its strategy. But few companies do consider the long term. Short-term thinking is endemic to modern business strategy. Let's look at an example of one industry that blinded itself and failed to think ahead: the American auto industry.

The Big Three Fuel Motown's Meltdown: A Failure to Sustain Profitability

Members of the U.S. Congress leaned forward as the big three American automobile executives raised their hands to vouch for the truth of their forthcoming testimony. The three—Ford Motor Company's CEO, Alan Mulally; General Motors Corporation's chair and CEO, Richard Wagoner; and Chrysler LLC's chair and CEO, Robert Nardelli—had flown separately on their private jets from Detroit, the birthplace of the automobile, to Washington, D.C. With hats in hand, they came to beg the American taxpayer to bail them out. "It's almost like seeing a guy show up at the soup kitchen in a high hat and tuxedo," quipped Representative Gary Ackerman, a Democrat from New York. "Couldn't you have downgraded to first class, or jet-pooled or something to get here?"[5]

Nardelli ignored the questions. He cut to the chase, explaining, "We are asking for assistance for one reason: to address the devastating automotive-industry recession caused by our nations' financial meltdown, and the current lack of consumer credit, which has resulted in the critical lack of liquidity within our industry." What about the dramatic changes over the last twenty-five years in transportation technology, consumer behavior, and human and natural resources that the U.S. automotive industry had not been addressing? House Republican leader John Boehner of Ohio asked as much a week before the fateful hearing: "Spending billions of additional federal tax dollars with no promises to reform the root causes crippling automakers' competitiveness around the world is neither fair to taxpayers nor sound fiscal policy."[6] Indeed, every strategy and action of these corporate titans and their counterparts at the major labor unions, particularly both parties' denial of the long-brewing causes of their current predicament, suggested a lack of connection to the changing world around them, changes that their foreign competitors seized to build long-term advantage.

The writing had been on the wall for the societal changes that have driven the current crisis. Had they learned nothing from the energy crisis in the 1970s? Or how about the first Gulf War and the signal that it sent that the developed and developing world would be fighting a perpetual military and economic war for oil and energy? Other heavily unionized industries in America had failed in the past, despite pleas at the time that they were "foundations of America." In industries from steel to textiles, corporate leaders formed a desperate alliance with union leaders and affixed themselves to a sinking ship, instead of committing to radical changes that would secure the industry's future.

The technological advances necessary to move the industry in the right direction had been around for twenty years or so. Lightweight carbon-fiber materials can dramatically increase the fuel efficiency of a car. Combine that with advances in "microelectronics, software, electricity-storage devices, [and] fuel cells" enabling "ultralight Construction, Low-Drag Design, Hybrid-Electric Drive, [and] Efficient Accessories" that outsiders like Rocky Mountain Institute had recommended, and Detroit had a roadmap for technological innovation.[7] All these ideas had been around before the spike in gas prices in the summer of 2008, when GM began trumpeting its Chevy Volt as the future of the company.

For the previous forty years, GM had seen its U.S. market share fall from 53 percent to 20 percent. Yet the company still had eight U.S. brands (Cadillac, Saab, Buick, Pontiac, GMC, Saturn, Chevrolet, and Hummer). As for its more successful competitors, Toyota (19 percent market share) had three, and Honda (11 percent) had two. GM had about seven thousand dealers. Toyota had fewer than fifteen hundred, and Honda had about a thousand.[8] This sort of scatter forced GM to overextend its marketing budget while still not saturating target audiences. Meanwhile, gas prices were going up, while Toyota and Honda's investments in hybrid technology led the way as an example of sustainable innovation. GM was already behind the curve by the time the credit crisis hit.

The Teamsters and the International Union, United Automobile, Aerospace and Agricultural Implement Workers of America (UAW) union are not without blame, either. The unions enabled a business-as-usual attitude in the Big Three. It was on the automakers' behalf that the Teamsters helped defeat environmentalists' attempts to protect the Arctic National Wildlife Refuge. Symbolically, the defeat was a statement that the automakers and the Teamsters would do whatever it took to maintain oil as their fuel of choice instead of changing directions to develop alternative sources of automotive energy. Together, the Big Three and the UAW loudly protested the U.S. government's push for more fuel-efficient cars through corporate average fuel economy (CAFE) standards and missed the signals of the coming resource shocks. During the great petroleum price spike in 2008, America's Big Three had a production advantage over their competitors only in light trucks and SUVs, precisely the cars consumers did not want.[9] The three automakers failed Detroit, their employees, their dealers, their shareholders, and their customers. By the time the three CEOs appeared on Capitol Hill, it seemed that everyone—no matter where he or she fell on the political spectrum— agreed that the American auto industry had to change how it did business, and fast.

But that was hindsight. What if the automakers had seen this firestorm coming years ago, and what if they had built and executed a strategy to avoid it altogether? That's what every business has the opportunity to do, today. There is a choice. Innovate differently, and win. Or continue to innovate narrowly, and lose—businesses can watch some savvy competitor pass them by as they scramble to recoup lost market share or, worse, fight for their very survival, as the American auto industry is doing. After the congressional hearing, Speaker of the House Nancy Pelosi declared, "Until they show us the plan, we cannot show them the money."[10]

This book is about how you can help any company craft such a plan much further upstream. It's about developing and executing a company's strategy that takes into account all aspects of sustainability but that is useful enough to be implemented today. It's about involving employees and the community in every part of the process. And it's about survival.

My advice—more precisely, my set of frameworks—has grown out of the two lessons I learned when I completely failed the City of New Orleans and when the automakers failed their stakeholders, employees, and customers. First, developing and executing a strategy for sustainability is critical for business's survival in today's rapidly changing world: one in which there are more hurricanes, fewer wet-lands, more limits on resources, and less credit to go around—and in which there will be more change tomorrow. Second, a successful strategy for sustainability is different from and much bigger than just "green": it must take into account every dimension of the environment in which your business operates—social, economic, and cultural, not just the natural environment.

No, a Green Strategy Is Not a Strategy for Sustainability

The word *sustainability* became widely used in an environmental context in 1987, after it appeared in a United Nations report by former Norwegian prime minister Gro Harlem Brundtland. Brundtland defined *sustainable development* as "meeting the needs of the present without compromising the ability of future generations to meet their own needs."[11] Before that time business leaders used the word "sustainability" to connote a company that had steady growth in its earnings.

A cashier in Indiana offered me this definition: "Sustainability is something I can do to take care of me and my family now, so that I don't make bad decisions that I'll have to deal with in the future."

Over time, the meaning of the word has become somewhat diluted. As Michael Pollan, author of *The Omnivore's Dilemma*, writes: "The word 'sustainability' has gotten such a workout lately that the whole concept is in danger of floating away on a sea of inoffensiveness. Everybody, it seems, is for it whatever 'it' means."[12] Pollan touches on the dark side of the interest in sustainability, a business phenomenon called *greenwashing*: when companies focus more on communicating their green efforts than improving their practices.[13]

Sustainability is also frequently used to describe the philanthropic efforts of an organization to protect the environment. Indeed, many business leaders file the word away in the part of their brain that deals with philanthropy, public relations, and compliance. Sure, these goals are necessary and valuable. But *sustainability* is not a buzzword or public relations stunt tacked on to your business. An environmental goal is not enough to manage a company's future successfully. Neither is an economic goal. In *Green to Gold*, Daniel Esty and Andrew Winston argued that smart companies should use environmental strategy to fuel business opportunities and innovation.[14] While they are quite right in identifying this new source of revenue, this economic goal itself should be only the first step toward a strategy for sustainability. The business argument for a comprehensive strategy for sustainability is not only that your company might make more on the top line or eliminate some costs to plump up the bottom line—it is that your company will survive and thrive by following emerging trends in society, technology, and natural resources.

For the purposes of this book, being a sustainable business means *thriving in perpetuity*. In this business context, sustainability is bigger than a public relations stunt, bigger than a green product line, bigger even than a heartfelt but part-time nod to ongoing efforts to save the planet. Imagined and implemented fully, sustainability drives a bottom-line strategy to save costs, a top-line strategy to reach a new consumer base, and a talent strategy to get, keep, and develop employees, customers, and your community. As I realized after Katrina, true sustainability has four coequal components:

- *Social* (acting as if other people matter): Actions and conditions that affect all members of society (e.g., poverty, violence, injustice, education, public health, and labor and human rights)

- *Economic* (operating profitably): Actions that affect how people and businesses meet their economic needs—for example, securing food, water, shelter, and comforts for people and for businesses turning a profit so that they'll be able to continue for years to come

- *Environmental* (protecting and restoring the ecosystem): Actions and conditions that affect the earth's ecology (e.g., climate change, preservation of natural resources, and the prevention of toxic wastes)

- *Cultural* (protecting and valuing cultural diversity): Actions through which communities manifest their identity and cultivate traditions from generation to generation

While there may very well be positive social, economic, and cultural benefits to a green strategy, they are not as integral to its success as they are to a strategy for sustainability. Let's look at an example. A green strategy might be to slow global warming by making energy more expensive. For example, on National Public Radio's *On Point*, Tom Ashbrook asked me and Auden Schendler, the executive director for community and environmental responsibility at Aspen Skiing Company and the author of *Getting Green Done*, whether gas should cost ten dollars a gallon to force people to conserve.[15] Such a tax would discourage consumers from driving and would thereby lower the amount of fuel consumed and the amount of carbon dioxide (CO_2) released into the atmosphere. In this case, the green strategy would succeed for the short term, but not be sustainable for the long term, because it would fail socially, economically, and culturally. Socially, because millions of people could not afford transportation to work, visit family, attend school, or participate in their community. Economically, because it would lower business output across the board—any industry that relied on transportation would be affected. And the strategy would fail culturally, because it would hit the poorest members of society the hardest—those who already had trouble affording the gas to get from one job to another, for example, further isolating wealthy, homogenous communities like Aspen, Colorado, from the changes on the rest of the planet.

Even as a green strategy, the idea of raising the price of gas to ten dollars a gallon would not work for long, since consumers would undoubtedly rebel and reject the tax. The sort of myopic view of green is similar to the myopic view of economic growth that many companies hold and that a broader strategy for sustainability would reject.

Now contrast that with Google's stated goal, the development of renewable energy cheaper than coal. As with the stated goal of the fuel tax, Google's plan would lower CO_2 emissions. But additionally, in the social sphere, the plan would bring millions of people who live in abject poverty to a higher quality of life. In the economic sphere, it would encourage low-polluting industries to expand over the long term without disrupting the private sector in the short term. And in the cultural sphere, the plan would make distances shrink as low-cost, low-pollution travel would bring new ideas into circulation across the world. So Google's plan is not just green, but also sustainable.

A Strategy for Sustainability for the Automobile Industry

Comparing Ford Motor Company's strategy and execution with that of Toyota Motor Corporation reveals what a measured and comprehensive strategy for sustainability might look like.[16] By May 2008, Ford's shareholders were restless. After years of promises of improved performance, the company was still losing money. CEO Alan Mulally knew he had to give context to the numbers. "Today," he said, "we have a lot of good news to share."[17]

He then explained that in 2007, Ford had an overall net loss of $2.7 billion. The loss was, however, significantly smaller than that of the previous year. Mulally had come from Boeing, where he was part of the team that had turned the company around to face the competitive challenge of Airbus. He had joined Ford to lead the "Way Forward," a strategy focused on reducing costs and capacity at the automaker, shuttering fourteen manufacturing plants by

2012, and laying off thirty thousand workers. He still had faith: "Our plan is working and we are sticking to it," he said in May.[18]

By November, after being smashed by three unforeseen waves—high gas prices, a credit crisis, and a recession—he had changed his opinion. "Much of the commentary I've read in the last few weeks is highly critical of our industry, and a common refrain is that our companies 'need a new business model.' I completely agree," he said at the congressional hearing as he sought a taxpayer backstop for the U.S. auto industry.

What had happened to this great company? In 1994, Ford was identified as a company with staying power.[19] Fifteen years later, it appeared to be on its last legs. Over the years, Ford had moved from a long-term strategy for sustainability to a short-term strategy for profitability. In 1907, Henry Ford had set a high-level aspirational goal that oriented the company, was aligned with its strengths, was personally actionable for everyone on board, and moved the company steadily but incrementally forward toward solving a global human challenge—a higher purpose than profit. Ford famously announced this lofty goal: "I will build a motor car for the great multitude . . . it will be so low in price that no man making a good salary will be unable to own one and enjoy with his family the blessing of hours of pleasure in God's great open spaces . . . When I'm through, everybody will be able to afford one, and everyone will have one. The horse will have disappeared from our highways, the automobile will be taken for granted . . . and we will give a large number of men employment at good wages."[20]

Compare this statement with the company's modern credo: "One team, one plan, one goal—one Ford—profitable growth for all."[21] Ford's focus had become survival, stopping the warring factions, returning to profitability. Its leaders had missed countless opportunities to respond to changes in society, technology, and natural and human resources to build a strategy for sustainability.

At the turn of the millennium, it seemed as if the company was heading in the right direction. In 2000, Jacques Nasser, then president and CEO of Ford, declared at the National Press Club that Ford would boost the fuel economy of its SUVs by 25 percent within five years.[22] Bill Ford, who would soon assume the top job, drove an electric Ford Ranger truck, and famed green architect William McDonough helped lead a $2 billion conversion of the company's Rouge assembly plant into one of the industry's greenest manufacturing facilities. But Ford would never achieve the 25 percent reduction in five years. Why? The environmental goals were peripheral to its core business strategy. What type of super-high-efficiency cars was it building under the green "living-roof" in the Rouge factory? The standard Ford F-150 gas-guzzling pickup trucks.

Even though Bill Ford's family owned 40 percent of the company, he wasn't able to translate the green strategy into a strategy for sustainability. The company was profiting on high-margin trucks and SUVs. There was little buy-in from the workers or the UAW to Ford's sustainability efforts. Crisis after crisis began occurring, from the Firestone tire recall to 9/11, causing the company to retrench and focus on the big vehicles, in which they had an advantage. Ford's first hybrid didn't hit the market until years after the Honda Insight and the Toyota Prius. Today, Ford CEO Alan Mulally is beginning to turn the company around; it was the only U.S. carmaker to not seek a direct Federal bailout and the vehicle quality has continued to improve. But did Ford wait too long to start striving for sustainability?

In contrast, Toyota's leadership followed a different path that placed sustainability into the core of its business strategy. Unlike Ford, Toyota was not losing money; in 2007, it reported record profits of $14.9 billion.[23] In the 1970s, Toyota had begun to focus on building quality small cars for export to the United States. U.S. manufacturers saw small, fuel-efficient cars as entry-level products and did not give them the quality features of full-sized cars. *Quality* became the watchword at Toyota. Says Katsuaki Watanabe, former Toyota chairman, "I am always saying that 'without improving quality, Toyota cannot expect to grow,' and I believe that quantitative growth is the result of improved quality."[24] Instead of focusing on one innovation to guide the company, Toyota focused instead on the so-called Toyota Way: "(1) Long-term thinking as a basis for management decisions, (2) adding value to the organization by developing its people, (3) a process for problem-solving, and (4) recognizing that continuously solving root problems drives organizational learning."[25]

Unlike Ford, Toyota has built its strategy around all four aspects of sustainability. Toyota's efforts to build a company that is harmonious with the changing needs of society led it to develop a balanced and diversified portfolio of cars. So while it has truck lines like the T100 and the Tacoma, those are balanced by the 1.5 million hybrid Prius cars that have been sold since 1997, with fleetwide fuel efficiency up by 17.4 percent in the decade since. Toyota understood how society's preferences were changing and reacted. It took the long view with economic sustainability as well; while Detroit put all its efforts into selling trucks, Toyota continued to develop hybrid technology, which paid off when gas prices spiked. Today, it plans to incorporate hybrid technology into all its cars by 2030.[26] It is not just Toyota's flagship hybrid Prius that is environmentally friendly; the company's equivalent to Ford's plant is the Tsutsumi plant, which has reduced its CO_2 emissions by 50 percent from the 1990 level and has a 2,000-kilowatt solar power plant.[27] As for the cultural aspects of sustainability, Toyota has shared the idea of the Toyota Way both inside the company and beyond. Management concepts like *genji genbutsu*, management by walking around and seeing for yourself; or *kaizen*, continuous improvement, have affected the management of companies worldwide. All of these come from a much broader goal than mere profitability. Former Chairman Watanabe said that he wanted to build cars that never crashed and that cleaned the environment as they drove. This leads the company toward new technologies like traffic analysis and rerouting software that will help Toyota reach its overarching goal, which lies far past the realm of profitability.[28]

Act Now: Make Today Count

In building a strategy for sustainability, companies must accept that a constant state of change is becoming the status quo. Sustainable organizations celebrate positive action in the face of bureaucracy and indifference. I titled my last book *Act Now, Apologize Later* to underscore how, when you are trying to do the right thing, acting and then asking for forgiveness is often more productive than asking for permission to act.

The movement toward sustainability is just getting started, and a few corporate leaders are rising to the challenge. The home-furnishing retailer IKEA has "air-hunters," people who search for empty space to reduce the size of packaging, and the merchandiser will stop giving out plastic bags and start selling solar panels and smart energy meters. Caterpillar, Inc., is now remanufacturing old engines to save raw materials and money.[28] After initially rebuffing remanufacturing, Caterpillar has become one of the largest engine remanufacturers in the world, recycling more than two million pounds of engines and transmissions into like-new components. The beer brewer Anheuser-Busch has committed to brewing five billion beers a year with renewable energy.[29] The U.K.-based food retailer J. Sainsbury Plc is printing double-sided register receipts with a simultaneous thermal printer from NCR Corporations, cutting paper consumption by 40 percent and saving accumulated hours of paper-roll replacement. The global airlines network International Air Transport Association no longer buys paper tickets, saving nine dollars of cost per flight.[30] Herman Miller Inc., the furniture maker based in Zeeland, Michigan, has reduced waste sent to the landfill by 80 percent, hazardous waste by 91 percent, overall emissions by 87 percent, and water usage by 67 percent, while doubling sales to more than $2 billion.[31] The list goes on.

The Chinese have a saying that the best time to plant a tree is a hundred years ago. The second-best time is right now. Sustainability has been lacking in modern business strategy. If your business has no strategy for sustainability, then its current strategy has already passed its sell-by date, and it's time to rethink your plans.

A strategy for sustainability differs from green strategy in scope and purpose—but if sustainability is so broad a strategy, what makes it different from how we think of business strategy now? Chapter 1 will begin by showing that several companies that were supposedly "built to last" were really not that sustainable after all—and will reveal a different approach to formulating a strategy that places long-term thinking at the core of the endeavor.

CHAPTER ONE

A Different Way to Formulate Your Business Strategy

C HAPARRAL DOMINATES the western coast of the United States, from the mountain slopes of the Rogue River Valley in Oregon to the hills of Baja, California.[1] Characterized by small, woody shrubs, the chaparral forest community survives the hot dry California summers by growing waxy coatings on leaves, building thicker cell layers on plants, and producing recessed *stomata*, the pores in leaves that permit evaporation. You can find these hobbit-like, hearty plants throughout similar climatic areas of the world, from South Africa to Spain.

As a child, I explored the scrubby chaparral behind my home in Southern California. Its resilience seemed magical. The red-hued trunk of a manzanita tree could survive a brush fire and sprout new branches the next year. The horned lizards could shoot blood from the sinuses in the corners of their eyes to defend themselves from coyotes. Yet this forest could not defend itself against human incursion. Four-thousand-square-foot track houses and eighteen hole golf courses spread out from Mulholland Boulevard through my small forest toward the foothills.

I watched the forest shrink and questioned why we were swapping a unique and natural environment for one common and largely artificial. Both offered social benefits: a field for kids to let their imaginations run wild in this elfin forest; a place for families to picnic and drink lemonade. Both environments provided cultural experiences: an exploration of a local ecosystem or a test of skill and confidence on well-sculpted terrain. But why destroy what nature itself might never replicate?

It led to a larger question: how did citizens and consumers of both culture and nature decide what to save and what to sacrifice? Why, I wondered, were Mozart, da Vinci, Kālidāsa, or Wang Bo, more precious, better insured, and better preserved than the chaparral, manzanita, and blood-shooting lizards? Over the years, I came to understand that both culture and nature are worthy of preservation and inextricably linked, but the immediate threats to the natural environment seemed more urgent at the time.

I realized—as one could not help realizing when Walmart's trucks delivered much-needed supplies to victims of Hurricane Katrina long before taxpayers' dollars did—that the effects of human activity on my childhood backyard and countless other distinct and irreplaceable ecosystems like the wetlands of New Orleans *could be positive*. Humans could save both people and planet. I began identifying the simple rules that nature follows to survive conditions far harsher than the worst market meltdown. Working *with* rather than *against* large corporations, which are members of ecosystems in their own right, I looked for strategic and operational solutions to their sustainability problems in the longest-running and still functioning system on Earth—the planet itself. That is why I call my approach to strategy simply a *strategy for sustainability*, though you could easily call it Earth's own strategy.

Nature's Simple Rules: The Basis of Strategy and Execution

We are constantly discovering new laws of nature and how humans, with our penchant for agriculture and technology, function within natural or legacy systems. Sometimes, we need only understand how a system works. I eat ice cream with the spoon facing down, not up, because there are more taste buds on my tongue than on the top of my mouth. Try it. Can you taste the difference?

Other times, we can adapt nature's lessons to our current technology. For example, mimicking the biomechanics of the wings of bats and dragonflies, Boeing Corporation put "winglets" on the wings of its 737 airplanes to reduce air resistance. Thousands of Boeing's 737s are now equipped with winglets. Every 737 with the winglets saves about 3 percent of its total fuel use. Across aviation, this will save billions of gallons of fuel.[2]

At the level of business strategy, scientists in the emerging fields of biomechanics, biomimicry, and biology are decoding rules that can help form businesses as hearty and long-lasting as a forest.[3] The rules, itemized in the epigraph at the opening of the book, hint at the flaws in current business strategy.

- Diversify across generations. Diversity in genetic makeup and behavior supports long-term species survival. Species differ widely across oceans.[4]

- Adapt and specialize to the changing environment. Natural organisms practice adaptive navigation, adjusting to changes in climate, food, and predators.[5]

- Celebrate transparency. Every species knows which species will eat it and which will not, which food is safe and which is not, and which species can help it.[6]

- Plan and execute systemically, not compartmentally. Nature creates solutions that optimize the system, not just individual components. But every organism in the system has knowledge built into its DNA. Animals instinctively survive and reproduce. Every part of a plant automatically contributes to its growth.[7]

- Form groups and protect the young. Most animals are not solitary; they travel in flocks, gaggles, and prides. Packs offer strength and efficacy. Nature obsesses over protecting its young.

- Integrate metrics. Nature brings the right information to the right place at the right time. When a tree needs water, the leaves curl. When it rains, the curled leaves move more water to the root system.[8]

- Improve with each cycle. Evolution can be harsh, but it's a strategy for long-term survival.[9] Recently, a frog without lungs was discovered. These cold-blooded amphibians don't need a lot of oxygen and can absorb it from the fast-moving oxygen-rich streams they live in, in Indonesia. Who would have thought a creature could evolve to lose a major organ?

- Rightsize regularly, rather than downsize occasionally. Organisms adjust to be as small or large as necessary; if an organism grows too big to support itself, it collapses. If it withers, it is eaten.

- Foster longevity, not just immediate gratification. Nature does not support unlimited growth or inefficient use of resources, but it does foster longevity. That means that it does not buy on credit and uses resources only to the level that they can be renewed, and adapts or dies when those resources run out.[10]

- Waste nothing, recycle everything, and borrow little. One organism's waste is another's food. Some of the greatest opportunities in the twenty-first century will be turning waste (inefficiency, underutilization, energy waste) into profit.[11]

As you can see, nature's rules for sustainability are social and economic as well as environmental. I add the cultural dimension to my definition so that we could consider the effects of our activity on the chaparral and on what makes us uniquely human. From Creole cultures to Charlie Parker to Spain's Corre Foc to the farming wisdom in a small Mayan village, human culture is as unique as a natural species. And yet today, we clear-cut our multiple cultures as surely as we clear-cut trees.

Seven Tenets of a Strategy for Sustainability

Nature's rules very much inform my business assumptions. I assume that our planetary resources are scarce, precious, and diminishing; that our human population is diverse, dispersed, and increasing; and that organizations must increase their internal and external transparency, engage their great repository of knowledge and talent, and connect more purposefully to their social, economic, environmental, and cultural (SEEC) systems.

So, before doing the situational analysis and scenario planning that underlie most companies' strategies, companies have the opportunity to rethink and challenge their own assumptions and the consequent practical implications for strategy. The model must not only factor in the following seven tenets but also include measures of the effects of each strategic alternative on the social, economic, environmental, and cultural systems. That means a different set of what-ifs and a multidimensional set of outputs.

1. Natural Resources Will Become Increasingly Scarce and Expensive.

Imagine if you had to open up a business on Mars. With only a thin atmosphere, the temperatures fluctuate from minus 140 degrees Celsius to a balmy 20 degrees Celsius, water is hard to come by, and the dust storms that blow in when Mars approaches the sun are so intense that the entire planet's climate changes. Whether it was divine intervention or cosmic luck, we're fortunate to have formed our civilization on the abundance of planet Earth.

Until recently, businesses have planned and implemented their strategies as if their natural resources were cheap, abundant, and easily accessible as long as the kingdom or country that claimed them was not hostile toward your kingdom or country. Such thinking drove many innovations of the industrial age. Now imagine if your company had to provide your employees and supply chain with the following resources or other benefits:

- Clean air to breathe

- Potable water

- Protection from ultraviolet light from the sun

- Protection from pests and exotic diseases

- Nutrient cycling (like nitrogen fixation and phosphorus cycles) to store, process, and break down nutrients

- Honeybees to pollinate flowers, and mice to carry seeds in their scat

- Predictable weather patterns that don't cause damage or delay

The list goes on and on. Most businesses today rely on inexpensive natural resources and high-functioning ecosystem services to bring their product to market. *Ecosystem services* are benefits provided by the natural ecosystem. They include natural resources like water, fuels, and plants; processes like decomposition, weather patterns, and nutrient cycling; and biological and genetic diversity. But few businesses are actually taking these benefits into full account in the formation of their strategy. All businesses require basic ecosystem services to function. According to an oft-quoted paper published in *Nature*, the total value of ecosystem services is about $33 trillion per year.[12] These are services that you depend on as surely as businesses depend on their accounting or customer relationship management (CRM) system, but for which they are not accounting.

The ecosystem provides fundamental services that we all take for granted. Some of these systems are propped up and maintained through common government or trade-industry action, but most ecosystem services are in grave danger of being overwhelmed by people's natural desire for an always-higher standard of living. In addition, the strain on nonrenewable resources like fossil fuels and metals means that prices will be at best wildly unpredictable and at worst prohibitively expensive.

Some companies have already adapted their business strategy toward the idea of sustainability in a turbulent planet of diminishing physical resources. For example, an increasing proportion of Xerox's business is now providing document services instead of copiers. It leases the machines and provides whatever a customer needs, including updating the technology. Xerox refurbishes the copier that you would otherwise discard. The result is higher customer satisfaction, lower energy usage, and a 91 percent rate of recycling of printers, demonstrating that you can minimize resource usage while maximizing service.

2. Massive Demographic Change Is Occurring.

Just as climate change is a slow-moving tsunami, so too is the rapidly growing population of the planet. The demographic reality of 3 billion more people on the planet by 2040, mainly where humanity has not achieved a stable standard of living, means that market dynamics will change rapidly in our lifetimes. Far from just considering the money to be made through microtransactions with the world's poor, businesses must integrate the changing consumer landscape into their strategies.

In so doing, we have the chance to deal with global inequities that destabilize business and society. For example, those of us in the developed world must share natural resources equitably with those in the developing world: which American can rightfully destroy twenty times more of the atmosphere than an African? Remember, most people on the planet still need more and better access to safe, reliable, and affordable energy supplies. These people bear an energy deficit—and that number is increasing daily. And so, businesses should not only look for opportunities to bring massive amounts of clean energy online, but also wean their operations from old, dirty energy sources.

Along with all these people will come even more diversity. Many of the most developed countries will find themselves with aging workforces and unable to manage their own pension and health liabilities. Meanwhile, consumer markets will mature in Asia, South America, and Africa. There, consumers will rightly begin demanding products made in ways that are culturally sensitive and keep a significant share of profits from their markets in the market itself. Big, global brands that demand strict uniformity in branding and materials must prepare to radically adapt their business model to serve local markets.

3. People Are the Most Important Renewable Resource.

Saying "Our people are our most important asset" is like saying that you believe that people should respect the wisdom of our elders. Yes, of course. But what are companies doing to care for and develop people, as nature would its young? What is their actual plan to protect and grow this asset as the most important part of an organization? One day during an executive immersion program at an InterfaceFLOR carpet plant in Georgia, a senior leader of a large multinational company asked a forklift driver for directions. "What's your job?" she asked after he had given her the directions. "My job is saving the planet," he said. Astonished by the answer, the executive began asking the Interface employee other questions about his experience at Interface. After a few minutes, the employee began showing increasing anxiety and finally said, "I'm sorry, ma'am. I have to go. Because if I don't get this delivered soon, it will slow down our line, making more waste and pollution, hurting the planet, not saving it." Now that's an engaged employee. Founded by chairman Ray Anderson, Interface has been a pioneer in placing sustainability at the core of its business model, reinventing and recycling carpet rather than creating it to be destroyed. The company's goal is to have zero impact on the planet, what it calls "Mission Zero." Mission Zero has become the center point of its external brand message and internal engagement programs around sustainability. The story comes from Jim Hartzfeld, one of the leaders of the green building movement and Interface, who now helps other companies imagine and move toward their own mission zero as well.[13]

Some companies use benefits to make the point. General Mills employees wait anxiously for the period of open benefits, when they can choose their benefits for the coming year. They know that any benefits offered, like the Total Health program, are best in class, and they do not want to miss that window of choice. One employee, Chuck Tryon, told me, "I know they care about me because of those benefits. It was a motivation to come and a motivation to stay."[14]

Some companies, like Google, invite their employees to participate in the innovation process. In the same way that 3M gave its engineers legendary freedom, Google allows its engineers to spend up to 20 percent of their time working on innovation projects.[15] At Live Labs, Microsoft's disruptive innovation campus, employees compete for "start-up" funding funneled to the best new initiatives.[16] Benefits or flexibilities aside, employees are the company, yet many leaders never tap into their full creativity and power.

Consider Circuit City, once the number two electronics retailer in the United States. In the 1980s and 1990s, it grew to over seven hundred outlets and over forty thousand employees.[17] Business pundits considered it a company that had gone from "good to great," partly by the company's policy of patiently waiting to fill the right position with the right person.[18] When asked to name the top five factors that led to the transition from mediocrity to excellence, vice president Walter Bruckart said, "One would be people. Two would be people. Three would be people. Four would be people. Five would be people."[19]

But the company's stock began falling, from thirty dollars per share in 2006 to ten cents in 2008. Neither the credit crunch nor the recession caused the fall: Circuit City began missing changes in society, technology, and resources. For example, its leadership decided to stop selling household appliances, forcing busy suburban families to shop wherever they could buy all their electronics instead of making a trip to a specialty store for a television and to another one for a microwave. It missed the Internet boom, dithering instead with proprietary technologies like DIVX while companies like Amazon.com transformed the customer experience. Above all, Circuit City badly managed its human resources, at one point firing its most experienced staffers to lower the average wages, leaving no reason for customers loyal to its expertise to visit Circuit City's locations. As CEO Philip J. Schoonover was pink-slipping his experts, he was pocketing $7 million in compensation.[20]

What happened? The company's human resource strategy failed. This loss of focus on engaging and maintaining a superior workforce was key to the retailer's decline. When nature rightsizes, it tends to weed out the weakest, not those with the most wisdom and experience. Moreover, Circuit City's actions provide a good metaphor for the type of short-term decisions that businesses make in a crisis and that tend to knock them into a death spiral. It is symptomatic of a short-term strategy for profitability. We experience the effects of "short-term-ism" every day, from managerial flame-outs that put beloved brands into bankruptcy seemingly overnight, environmental degradation, and worker unrest, to violent market gyrations, unpredictable commodity prices, and intransigent social problems.

4. Cash Flow Matters More Than Quarterly Earnings.

At one time in our civilization, military leaders instructed their troops to fire off inventory of ammunition to avoid losing it in the budget review for the coming year. How do your business's budgeting process and practices differ today? Responding to stock markets, public companies set the fiscal year's budget and then obsess maniacally over quarterly earnings to demonstrate superior performance. The ends of quarters and the end of a fiscal year can take on a Monte Carlo feel, with money either sloshing about or completely withheld, depending on expenses. One multibillion-dollar global company I know has a travel and entertainment (T&E) expense freeze every fourth quarter. Another large company regularly enforces a hiring freeze between July and February to contain costs. Cross your fingers that top talent searches for a new job in the first half of your fiscal year.

Even though every business school teaches that a company derives its value from the present value of its future cash flows, analysts continue to use quarterly earnings as the single determinant of a firm's health. Michael Mauboussin's work for Legg Mason Capital Management has shown that the gap between valuations and future cash flows is substantial. He recounts that in one catalog of sell-side analyst reports, 99.1 percent mention earnings and price-to-earnings multiples, while only 12.8 percent use some variation of discounted cash flow to derive target prices.[21]

Focusing on earnings leads to unsustainable business for at least three reasons, all of which relate to slippery metrics and the lack of transparency. First, earnings do not account for the cost of capital, and so there is no absolute link between the growth in earnings per share and the building of shareholder value. Second, earnings can be calculated in several ways, all of which are equally acceptable, according to current accounting standards. Companies can account differently for inventory and depreciation, for example, which can radically alter the appearance of their earnings. Third, earnings do not include additional capital that a company will need for future growth.

Some investors would argue that the daily valuation of the markets imposes discipline on a company's management, effectively leveraging and growing its capital, but this view undermines the long-term responsibility that managers have as stewards of the company, its customers, its employees, and its community. One study showed that 80 percent of the executives polled said they would forgo a value-creating project to present smooth earnings.[22]

This quarterly focus also tends to constrict innovation cycles to a shorter time horizon, so that the innovations that do appear are quick wins rather than game changers. Consequently, these premature innovations merely catch up to competitors and neutralize their advantage instead of creating the breakthroughs that create long-term business growth. Sony, for example, has been caught in this cycle and seems to be stuck trying to neutralize competitor advantage through the Sony Walkman version of the iPod or the Sony e-Book reader, which is a poor cousin to the Amazon.com Kindle.

"Green" change efforts tend to fit nicely in a quarter-focused company, because the efficiency projects resemble other quality improvements, noteworthy in a handsome annual sustainability report. But these small efforts toy on the fringe of opportunity, where immediate results matter more than breakthrough progress.

Before the 2008 global stock market crash, short-term incentives for executives kept increasing, while incentives for the sustainability of the company continued to erode. Up-front deal fees became standard, wherein brokers would get paid on the basis of consummating the deal rather than the success of the project. Meanwhile, private capital, the so-called last vestige of patient capital, began going public. These large sums of investment capital rapidly became enmeshed in the same type of quarter-by-quarter focus that can be so destructive to building a long-term company.

5. Every Organization's Operating Environment Will Change as Dramatically in the Next Three to Five Years as It Has Changed in the Last Five.

In the current business strategy model, tinkering with your core business strategy is like changing your engine while driving down the road. Some CEOs provoke a crisis so that people will pull the car over and will realize that something must change. But most often, strategy is formed while normal operations continue, even though the current strategic design process—where you stop everything and review—is ill-suited for this.

Like it or not, we are in a period of historic change, in which the pace and scale of those changes dwarf our past experience. Strategic planning must be much more dynamic in this future, with contingencies and, more importantly, organizational flexibility to react when the challenge occurs. This flexibility is core to a strategy for sustainability.

The American auto industry found itself existentially challenged by high oil prices that pushed American consumers toward highly fuel-efficient cars, a category in which American car companies have not traditionally excelled. After taking an inordinately long time to react to this new reality, the companies mustered their efforts into cars like the plug-in Chevy Volt. Yet just as they were getting some traction for this new strategy, they were hit by the credit crisis and the resulting belt tightening by the American consumer. It was as if the automakers were knocked down by a wave on the beach, and as they stood up, they were smacked back down by two more waves. They had planned to react to the first wave, but had not anticipated additional massive change.

The implication is straightforward: your process for developing strategy must accommodate nonlinear, lockstep change. Traditional strategy making and executing is linear. There are a number of different models for how companies form their strategy, but most strategic processes boil down to the following sequence of steps:

Discover—Assess the business context, establish a mission, a vision, and values.

Define—Define competitive advantage, and establish goals.

Plan—Translate the strategy into an operations plan with measurable objectives.

Execute—Execute with cult-like passion and excellence.

Measure—Measure, review, and refine.

The preceding list is what traditional, great gurus of strategy might call a "ready, aim, fire" approach to strategy. Internet gurus advised businesses to accelerate the process, advising strategists simply to "Aim, fire! Aim, fire!" But in today's chaotic world, you cannot wait to complete one step before you start the next. Sustainability calls on businesses simply to "fire." Businesses must adapt constantly. Instead of trying to be right with every decision, organizations need to empower themselves to make thousands of decisions and accept that they'll make some mistakes in the process.

This tactic is necessary because the time horizon for strategic development is getting shorter. Just as politicians today run a "perpetual campaign" to govern with a continuing intensity and focus on communications, strategic change needs to be a part of the everyday functioning of all companies. They can't just wait for their every-eighteen-month offsite. Strategy must be a living organism, confident in what will stay the same and prepared to change everything else.

6. A Chaotic External World Requires Internal Cohesion and Flexibility.

At their founding, companies must connect with the human need that they are solving. As they mature, they often lose touch with the outside need and fall into a moat of circular logic that protects them from criticism. It goes, "We are an acknowledged leader in our industry because we excel at what we do. Addressing your feedback is impossible in our current strategic paradigm and/or business model, therefore we must reject it, thank you profusely, and keep doing what we are doing because we can afford to, as an acknowledged leader in the field."

From an ecological standpoint, few companies can "go it alone," regardless of their internal capacities or resources. The challenges will be too great. From a consumer-insight perspective, no company can function and not know what the customer is feeling. Thinking more broadly, you can't ignore what those who affect the customer perceive. You can't be disconnected from trends in society and believe that those trends won't quickly invade your customer relationships.

At your local retailer, you can still find many products that do not have a customer comment number on them. Without customer input, how can a company know whether its product is fulfilling the customers or just placating them until your competitor comes around? How do you know when your product is making people sick? How do you know if your packaging is ruined when the customer takes it home? How do you know when your consumer has an idea for you to improve?

To maintain internal flexibility that allows your company to be in a constant state of change, a strategy must engage every part of the system—every person on staff, every supplier in the chain. Strategies fail more often because of poor implementation than because of poor strategic decisions. Yet, too often, organizations consistently agonize over choosing a great idea and not over implementing it. (Who would not want to go to the moon? But how to get us there?)

Does this sound familiar? An executive team books a day offsite at an expensive location, perhaps with high-priced, provocative consultants who help the team erect their strategic framework. They bond. They play golf. They return from the retreat, triumphant, and declare the new strategy. They send out a memo. They hold a large meeting. Their change effort fizzles.

One midlevel executive from a large household goods producer told me that his colleagues are so familiar with this experience that when his company was acquired, the staff from the acquired company signed e-mails "TTWP." What does TTWP mean? "This too will pass." TTWP is a symptom of initiative fatigue, caused by new initiatives with little long-term commitment from senior leadership and without a clear connection to a widely experienced problem. If the team members believe that this is just another flavor of the month, then they'll have no success at breaking through the natural inertia in an organization. Organizations with high initiative fatigue frequently suffer from the failure to build a powerful leadership coalition and lack an engagement effort that connects the initiative to the daily routines of the affected employees.

7. Only the Truly Transparent Will Survive.

Opacity is the enemy of sustainability (and, as we have witnessed lately, an incubator of managerial paranoia, incompetence, isolationism, and corruption). You must have pertinent, accessible, and engaging information readily available inside and outside the organization. Scary? You bet. But the death of your company or your career is scarier, right? Far too many initiatives fail because of the lack of basic communication inside the organization about how the strategy will work, how it will improve performance, and what role each person should play. Easy information is the core lubricant of this process. It is not really a question of whether the information exists or whether a company has attempted to communicate that information; the question is whether the information has successfully been integrated into practice and belief.

A cultural acceptance of opacity in the business world allows complexity to take precedence over common sense. Take, for example, the practice of splitting mortgages into tranches of statistically modeled debt-risk profiles that could "never lose." When marketed to investors, their prospectuses were hundreds of pages long and completely impenetrable. When layered with bogus insurance represented in credit default swaps, the proposition became even more opaque and the contracts were effectively void because so few people understood what they meant. So when panic hit and investors didn't know what they owned, it was inevitable that the largest credit default swap owners, companies like AIG, would fail. A cultural acceptance of a lack of transparency allowed the company to fail.

Good, timely information allows each person to do his or her share and to personalize the change initiative to match each person's own goals and objectives. This sort of free exchange of information builds simple memes and myths that are critical for organizational adoption.

To summarize, the seven tenets of a strategy for sustainability are:

1. Natural resources will become increasingly scarce and expensive.

2. Massive demographic change is occurring.

3. People are the most important renewable resource.

4. Cash flow matters more than quarterly earnings.

5. Every organization's operating environment will change as dramatically in the next three to five years as it has changed in the past five.

6. A chaotic, external world requires internal cohesion and flexibility.

7. Only the truly transparent will survive.

Formulate Your Strategy for Sustainability

In the remainder of this book, I will walk you through a rough process and some successful practices for building sustainability into the core of any company's operations. I say "rough" because at least for now, the best strategies for sustainability come about in highly messy, decentralized, bottom-up ways, where entrepreneurs like Anita Roddick (The Body Shop), Yvon Chouinard (Patagonia), and Gary Erickson (ClifBar) create a company to complete a "get us to the moon" mission, hire people who care about that mission, and then unleash their talent and passion to figure out how to complete it. Or sometimes, it's one frontline employee who pushes a part of the business to become more sustainable. The process is not unlike what flight director Gene Kranz did when the crew of Apollo 13 experienced colossal trouble en route to the moon. The mission was clear: save Apollo 13. Ongoing communications with crew members, their families, government officials, and the media kept the constraints and the opportunities transparent, focused everyone on the ultimate goal, and helped prioritize activities and the use of resources. Calling on its vast network of engineers, manufacturers, and other experts who could possibly help complete the mission, management engaged professionals on the ground to ideate, select and test options, document the best process, guide implementation, and monitor results. It was messy—but it worked.

So I am proposing a rough guide for instigators of change who want to understand what they are getting themselves into before they proceed. But some ideas in this guide are original here, and some are not. Building any business strategy requires analyzing the changing landscape and engaging in scenario planning. If you share my business assumptions—that the human world is changing more rapidly now than it ever has—then you need a planning process that is fast, nimble, easily understood, and focused on change. Such tools as a SWOT analysis, wherein you chart your strengths, weaknesses, opportunities, and threats, or an in-depth PESTEL analysis, which looks at the politics, your environment, society, technology, the economy, and your legal framework, are both valid, yet too slow and cumbersome for our purposes.

I prefer to analyze the micro and macro changes in society, technology, and natural resources through a rapid analysis that I call *STaR mapping*. For example, the Ford Motor Company faced a number of changes that were only exacerbated by the economic downturn and the credit crunch. Each change could be analyzed as a STaR element:

- *Social changes*: Ford's health-care costs spiraled out of control, yet it sought no government action to put U.S. automakers on a competitive playing field with foreign competitors.

- *Technological changes*: While its competitors innovated in high-efficiency vehicles, Ford redoubled its investment in short-term, high-margin sports utility vehicles rather than push for better distribution and environmental standards for ethanol so that Ford could promote its smaller flex-fuel Fiesta and EcoSport in the United States.[23]

- *Resource changes*: Price spikes in oil rapidly shifted consumer demand and rendered the operating costs of most Fords out of reach of the average consumer. As funding for consumer loans grew scarce, Ford found itself unable to move its more efficient automobiles.

We will look at more sophisticated examples of STaR mapping in chapter 2, which provides a battery of questions that any business could ask about each area and discusses how to identify the biggest threats and opportunities. STaR mapping places less emphasis on competitive analysis and more on discovering the little steps you can take today throughout the organization.

You must also articulate what I call a distinct *North Star goal*, the strategic direction toward which an organization drives to reach greater sustainability. By North Star goals, I mean goals that have these attributes:

- They move steadily but incrementally forward toward solving a global human challenge; they address a purpose larger than any company.

- They align with and benefit from an organization's strengths.

- They are achievable in five to fifteen years.

- They are personally actionable; everyone on board contributes to progress.

- They are both optimistic and aspirational, but not impossible.

- They connect to the core business; they are not tangential or bolted on.

- They ignite individuals' passion in your organization.

Like a Christopher Columbus, you must point to the destination—say, the Indies—even though you have no idea how to get there over water. Your people will figure out how to cast off, when to shift sails, and how to move the organization forward. Like Columbus, if you are open to discovery, you may reach an unexpected new world. Is it one without illiteracy or disease? Is it one with breathable air, drinkable water, and equality of resources, shelter, and food? And what will you learn from the people there?

In chapter 3, we will look at how companies like Procter & Gamble and Stonyfield Farm determined their North Star goals and identified the initial actions necessary to mobilize their people, open up their information and communications channels, and engage their whole network of suppliers, customers, and community *even before* they decided which product, service, or other idea to pursue. Here is what traditional managers struggle to understand, and so I will repeat it: you must first move toward greater transparency, deep employee engagement, and a stronger network support as prerequisites to idea generation, selection, and implementation. Chapters 4, 5, and 6 demonstrate initial steps to (1) opening up information so that employees and everyone else in your network can analyze the current business with regular STaR mapping, (2) engaging employees with different teamwork, longer-term incentives, and other programs, and (3) embracing and managing the contributions of your network. These three initiatives, transparency, engagement, and networking—the TEN cycle—are so called because they work cyclically to renew the conditions under which you can prosper in the long term and achieve your North Star goals. Table 1-1 shows how the actions of strategists for sustainability and those for profitability differ in STaR mapping and the TEN cycle.

In a rapidly changing context, thriving depends on how people behave, how they use their tools of analysis and execution, and how

TABLE 1-1

Tools for developing strategy

Strategy tool	What strategists for sustainability do	What strategists for profitability do
STaR Map	• Integrate short-term objectives with long-term strategy • Base plans on unpredictable energy and commodity costs • Build for a 9-billion-person world with aging populations in many of the richest economies in the world • Plan for change	• Maniacally focus on the results of the quarter and the year • Rely on inexpensive natural resources to bring product to market • Ignore that the world will have 3 billion new people by 2040 • Assume that the external environment will stay the same for three to five years
TEN Cycle	• Celebrate transparency • Build from the inside out • Demonstrate that "our people are our most important asset" • Provide deep induction processes and long-term equity incentives for employees • Stay highly networked to outside organizations and companies • Employ cyclical, constant actions	• Hold information tight • Trickle from the top down • Pay only lip service to "our people are our most important asset" • Offer short-term incentives for employees • Ignore world outside the company walls • Employ linear, periodic actions

they lead and align under uncertainty. Chapter 7 examines the kind of leadership necessary to orchestrate all these elements. It showcases leaders from companies like Xerox, method, and Seventh Generation. Without an overarching mission, without internal connections to each member of your organization and external connections to everyone who needs you or feeds you, and without full disclosure and communication to increase your unit's transparency, you stand little chance of leading your company through a hurricane. Instead of fortifying and digging in deeper against a storm, you must be flexible and resilient. See "Does 'Built to Last' Mean 'Sustainable'?"

Being an instigator for a strategy for sustainability will not be easy. In the pages that follow, you'll read stories of companies that are heading in the right direction, but that still have a long way to

Does "Built to Last" Mean "Sustainable"?

PEOPLE OFTEN ASK ME how companies that are pursuing a strategy for sustainability differ from companies
that were deemed *built to last*, a phrase defined by James C.
Collins and Jerry I. Porras in *Built to Last: Successful Habits
of Visionary Companies*. Reverse-engineering the success
of these companies, Porras and Collins compiled a series of
proverbs and practices to help managers sustain their businesses. Be a clock builder, not a timekeeper, they counseled,
because built-to-last companies "concentrate primarily on
building an organization—building a ticking clock—rather
than on hitting a market just right with a visionary product
idea and riding the growth curve of an attractive product life
cycle."[a]

There are indeed similarities in the habits of built-to-last
companies and those pursuing sustainability. For example,
both types of companies focus on both short- and long-
term achievements, develop organizational capabilities to
innovate and respond to change, cultivate multiple generations of chief executives, survive multiple product or service
life cycles over several decades. (See table 1-2 for a comparison of such characteristics with those founded on nature's
simple rules.)

Out of the eighteen companies profiled as built to last,
Boeing, Sony, Merck, Motorola, Citibank, and Ford have all
struggled to keep up with Standard & Poor's 500. Motorola
pioneered the cellular telephone, Global System for Mobile
Communications standard, digital cellular technology, and
e-mail through two-way pagers. But failing to see that society was becoming ever more mobile, the company sat by as

TABLE 1-2

Comparison of a built-to-last strategy with a strategy for sustainability

Built to last*	Sustainable
Definition of visionary	
A premier institution in its industry and one that (1) maintains a strong reputation, (2) contributes positively to society, (3) was founded before 1950, (4) concentrates on building an enduring institution, (5) pursues core ideology and not just profits, (6) adapts without compromising its cherished core ideals, (7) commits to "Big, Hairy, Audacious Goals," (8) grows its own management, (9) hires according to its core ideology, and (10) experiments strategically	An organization that (1) forms groups, that is, supports families and communities, not just employees and customers, (2) "rightsizes," adjusting its resource consumption and production to be as small or large as necessary, (3) embraces diversity of all kinds, (4) turns waste into profit and does not dump in its neighborhood, (5) evolves with each generation of products, processes, and people, (6) does not buy on credit, using resources only to the level and at the rate that they can be renewed, (7) optimizes its systems, not just its individual components, (8) has good metrics and information transparency, and (9) adapts quickly to changes to the environment, resources, and competition
Type of leadership	
Clock builders, not timekeepers, people who build on the organization's "core value system" instead of relying on great product ideas or their own charisma to achieve short-term results	Servant-leaders who are both clock builders and timekeepers, but who recognize how today's actions will serve the next generation
Leadership focus	
Manage to founder's core values, balancing quarterly profitability with perpetual viability and embracing the "genius of the 'And,'" that is, managing seeming extremes such as low cost and high quality	Connect with and manage to core values of broader global challenges (societal, economic, environmental, and cultural) and not just those of the founder or the organization
Driving business goals	
"Big, Hairy, Audacious Goals": clear, compelling, imaginative, tangible, achievable, and bold; take revolutionary steps forward; guide strategy development and unify efforts, fuel progress, rally staff, and require real stretch	"North Star goals": optimistic, aspirational, achievable in five to fifteen years, and personally actionable; connect to the core business and a larger purpose; ignite individuals' passion in the organization; are incremental steps to solve a global human challenge; and align with organization's strengths

(continued)

TABLE 1-2   (CONTINUED)

How to think about trade-offs

Tyranny of the "Or"	All four elements of sustainability—social, economic, environmental, and cultural—essential

Organizational culture

Cultlike, wherein employees believe strongly in the company's core ideology and managers indoctrinate or fire employees who do not fit; elitist; an arrogance of membership in such a visionary company; information held tight	Open, welcoming, transparent, and driven by a larger purpose; employees experience a confluence between personal and work lives; employees understand organization's role in and obligation to larger world

Tools for constant

"Preserving the core and stimulating progress": the evolutionary process as "branching and pruning," that is, if you "add enough branches to a tree (variation) and intelligently prune the deadwood (selection), then you will more likely evolve into a collection of healthy branches better positioned to prosper in an ever-changing environment"; product lines, profit strategies, cultural tactics, and organization structure can change—but a core ideology should not	Ongoing STaR (society, technology, and resources) mapping of changes; ongoing TEN (transparency of information; engagement of employees; and network of suppliers, customers, investors, and both local and global community) cycle management; scenario analysis of specifically how potential changes in STaR will affect the SEEC (social, economic, environmental, and cultural) goals of one's strategy, relative to organizational behavior

*Quotations in the "Built to Last" column are from James C. Collins and Jerry I. Porras, *Built to Last: Successful Habits of Visionary Companies* (New York: Collins Business, 2004).

competitors such as Palm, Research in Motion (RIM), and Apple developed devices that helped people manage their more complex lives. Motorola also failed to innovate on the production processes for its phones, leading to a large spill of a potential carcinogen into the Scottsdale, Arizona, water supply.[b] Similarly, Boeing failed to meet the needs of its constituents; union strife shut its plants down three times in a decade.[c] Moreover, the high cost of jet fuel diminished the profits of, and plane orders from, its largest customers, the airlines. Boeing's recent efficiency efforts are now heading in the right direction. The pharmaceutical giant Merck faced more than the Vioxx recall: advances in technology have resulted in increased competition from other firms, including those making generics. More dire is Merck's failure to address the underlying societal problems behind the diseases it treats; its drugs counter the effects of bad eating habits (such as high cholesterol and diabetes), but not the habits themselves. And there are plenty of other examples. These companies may have been built to last, but their strategies have not proved to be sustainable.

It's not that those companies lacked the internal qualities necessary for success, but that many firms were missing the ability to react to changes in their external business context. Behavioral economists describe this phenomenon as *fundamental attribution error*, the tendency to ascribe success or failure to personality or organizational characteristics and devaluing the overall context within which that performance functions.

Built-to-last characteristics make for a strategy for profitability. To be profitable for the long term, a company must first be sustainable, and sustainability in uncertain times means developing extraordinary connections to the world outside a company. It means recognizing that natural resources are finite and costly and the world's demography is exploding. And unless a company first opens itself up toward greater transparency, engages all of its employees equally, and embraces its network of suppliers, customers, and community—that company's leaders *will come up with a truly unsustainable strategy or are likely to execute a decent strategy poorly*.

a. *Built to Last* (New York: Collins Business, 2004), 23.

b. When Motorola accidentally dumped trichloroethylene (TCE, a potential carcinogen) into the Scottsdale water supply, five thousand people were unable to get tap water for three days. Diana Balazes, "Companies Trying to Prevent PV Water Pollution," *Arizona Republic*, 9 May 2008, www.azcentral.com/news/articles/2008/05/09/20080509sr-pvwater 0510-ON.html.

c. The strikes occurred in 1995, 2000, and 2005.

go. How will you know when you arrive? The ultimate test of sustainability comes during crisis, at which time the wind will fill the sails you've built. But in the meantime, the small steps you can start today will begin creating incremental gains. Still, pointing a company toward long-term thinking will feel risky if you are doing it right. Most of your competition does not think this way, so prepare yourself for ridicule. But the fearful often mock and fight great ideas before accepting them. Anyone who claims to know the one true path for a business is probably wrong. So you might as well get started.

CHAPTER TWO

Mapping Your Opportunities

An Analysis of Society, Technology, and Resources (STaR)

TSUKIJI MARKET IN TOKYO is a whirling mass of giant fish hauled from the depths of the ocean. Continuously operated since the Edo period, it is the largest fish market in the world. Its fishmongers, dressed in pale blue shirts, dark blue pants, and black wader boots, smoke filterless cigarettes and joke among themselves as large tuna sell for $10,000, $20,000, even $30,000 per fish. The men finish the auctions by six o'clock each morning. Fathers work beside their sons to slice the tuna with swordlike knives as they have done for generations. The speed, size, and efficiency of the market are stunning.

To prepare for my first visit to Tsukiji, I read the work of Boris Worm of Dalhousie University in Nova Scotia. His meta-study, published in *Science,* showed that 29 percent of fish species had been affected by overfishing, habitat destruction, or pollution and were in what scientists call *a state of collapse*, which is defined as a 10 percent or greater drop in population from its previous level.[1] Worm carried the trend forward to predict that the entire global ocean fishery would enter a state of collapse by 2048.[2]

So how was Tsukiji responding to this imminent threat? Its prices have risen, thanks to the increased scarcity of fish and society's growing demand for this food resource. Fish now accounts for 16 percent of the average protein diet globally, and fish consumption has doubled since 1973.[3] Modern technologies, from radar to nets, have enabled people to catch fish more efficiently further out in the ocean. Thousands of the ocean's last giant fish continue to move through the market each day. As a key distribution choke point in the global fish market, Tsukiji could advocate for sustainable fish harvesting, which would guarantee both the future employment of the market participants and Tsukiji's relative importance in the global fish marketplace. Instead, Japan has fought to maintain the current fishing system. So unless someone else intervenes or Tsukiji's many participants—including sushi lovers, like me—agree to change our behavior, Tsukiji's whole system will collapse, bringing down the fish market and thousands of jobs with it.

Contrast Tsukiji's unsustainable situation with that of the Pacific halibut, prized by chefs for its moist, white meat. The fish's population around Alaska had been declining throughout the twentieth century. Regulators had tried to shorten the length of the fishing season as the Pacific halibut population fell, but this did little to halt the population decline. Technology conspired with human ingenuity to increase the catch. The number of boats increased, as people worked almost twenty-four hours a day during the short season to catch fish. By the time the industry finally came together to change, the season was a frenzied eight days long. Participants agreed to a permit system that limited to sustainable levels the total amount of fish that could be caught. Today, halibut is available year round, and its population is increasing. We can enjoy halibut for decades to come.[4]

So how will you react to such changes in supply and demand and the capabilities of society, technology, and natural resources, relative to your business ecosystem? Will you ignore the threats as the players of the Tsukiji market have and fight against reform? Or will you step up as the fishers of Pacific halibut have and ensure your sustainability?

As introduced in chapter 1, STaR mapping—the mapping of the opportunities that arise out of changes in society, technology, and resources—is a critical component to a more sustainable response, and this chapter will get you started. Let's first look at what a more traditional business did to identify its threats and to map its opportunities.

Green Works Natural Cleaners, by The Clorox Company

Perhaps the most surprising recent commercial sustainability innovation has been produced by a company known for its bleach, the Oakland, California–based Clorox Company. Clorox effectively navigated changes to the external context in ways that will ensure its long-term sustainability.

Clorox was founded in early May 1913 by five Californians who invested a hundred dollars apiece to start their venture.[5] Their plan was to turn brine from the San Francisco Bay into bleach. The business struggled at first until a new general manager, William C. R. Murray, steered the company toward making a less concentrated bleach solution for home use. Murray's wife, Annie, who ran a grocery store in Oakland, began giving away free samples of the household bleach in fifteen-ounce amber glass "pints" with a 5.25 percent sodium hypochlorite solution that worked as a laundry additive to disinfect clothes and make them whiter.

Although Clorox spokespeople are quick to say that household bleach is safe when used according to the manufacturer's directions, changes in society were clearly creating an increased demand for products based on natural ingredients. Public demand for non-toxic products is growing exponentially. This was not always the case. When Clorox bleach was first formulated, the sole concern of consumers was how well it cleaned. Today, some consumers expect companies to produce goods that perform with natural ingredients. Clorox reacted to this change in society rather than defending the status quo. But it needed a business opportunity to make it real. That opportunity came in the form of a new CEO.

In 2006, when Don Knauss became CEO of The Clorox Company, he actively declared his desire to bring about bold change. Appraising Clorox's $4.4 billion in sales, he set out to create a new growth strategy that would enlarge the company in time for its hundredth anniversary in 2013.[6] The strategy was to focus on creating products for two megatrends: wellness and sustainability. Bill Morrissey, the vice president of environmental sustainability for Clorox and a veteran leader with twenty-five years' experience in the business, was tapped to lead the overall sustainability initiative, even though he was not a granola-eating environmentalist. "I knew the business and how to get things done," he said. Morrissey believed Clorox needed to "hitch our wagons to the megatrends if we wanted to see the growth we needed."[7]

This was not a company in dire need of change. Clorox had seen steady growth; dividends had been paid without interruption since 1968. But with commodity prices rising—and people becoming more interested in natural ingredients—Clorox knew it would have to position itself for the future.

What Changes in Society Meant for Clorox

Clorox had dealt with society's changing expectations before 2006. In 1957, Procter & Gamble (P&G) purchased Clorox. The acquisition was challenged in the U.S. Supreme Court, which ruled in 1969 that it violated antitrust statutes, forcing Clorox to stay independent after a decade of distraction surrounding the merger. Some thirty-five years later, society's expectations had changed, the prices of the bleach's ingredients had skyrocketed, and new technology had made it possible for natural ingredients to clean as effectively as their chemical predecessors.

Once Clorox decided to enter the sustainability world, it needed to map the opportunities so that it would be consistent with its core strengths and core values. Its first move was to expand the marketing of Brita water filters and reposition Brita as a sustainability brand. Brita was a brand that was growing nicely, but it had never been promoted as a sustainability solution. After all, the brand responded to societal desire to drink safe water, the technological ability to purify water on your own countertop, and the blatant resource use (both solid waste and consumer dollars) spent on billions of disposable plastic bottles. Seeing this confluence, Clorox began telling Brita's story. The company produced advertisements showing that one Brita filter could save the equivalent of three hundred disposable water bottles.

Today, Brita's sustainability story goes a step further. The team found a way to recycle the filters after use through a program with Preserve, a company that makes other household products out of No. 5 polypropylene plastic, a primary material in Brita pitcher filters.

Around 2004, a few product scientists at Clorox had begun working on natural ingredients as cleaning agents and began to find some intriguing results. Jessica Buttimer, who had already spent years marketing cleaning products, pulled together a team to investigate whether "natural" could spark a new product line.

Buttimer, a mother of two young children, lives in the redwood- and activist-filled hills of Marin County on the other side of the Golden Gate Bridge from San Francisco. A veteran of Clorox and P&G, she had always been a business innovator and had years earlier tried to launch a "natural" kitty litter line that was flushable and biodegradable. "The world just wasn't ready for it, I guess," she said.[8]

The team's first effort was to create a natural cleaner that worked. "There were some people who were skeptical that we could get a natural cleaner to be as effective as a conventional cleaner," said Buttimer. "And when we got our first tests back, it did not work as well as we had hoped. So we went back and worked on it some more." It had been more than twenty years since Clorox had launched a new brand, and the team members wanted to get it right. They knew that society was putting pressure on parents to keep a clean house while never threatening the health of their children with harsh chemicals. Buttimer and her team knew that they had the opportunity to develop technology that would provide the same cleaning strength offered by conventional cleaners.

They faced a number of challenges. The first was to understand why people were not buying natural cleaning products. "We started by listening to women across the country, and we found an unmet need for natural cleaners," Buttimer said. She found that a lot of people said they wanted natural cleaners, but their behavior at the store was different. When the team started its research, only 1 percent of consumers were actively looking for green cleaning products—a niche far too small for a company the size of Clorox. The team pressed ahead, confident that the market would mature. It set about studying what was keeping consumers from buying natural products and identified four major impediments:

1. Consumers did not think the products worked.

2. The products were too expensive.

3. Consumers could not find the products.

4. Consumers were not sure if they could trust the brand.

"It was clear the barriers to trial were pretty high," said Buttimer. She and her coworkers realized that to reach this audience, they needed a different angle. "This was something that communications couldn't handle alone. It was clear we needed to have a product approach."

They also found a number of motivators for using green products, ranging from altruism to cost savings to status to personal protection. Altruism—doing the right thing with no personal benefit—was the lowest-scoring of these four qualities in their research. The highest-scoring was personal protection: doing things that protect "me and my family."[9]

In scanning the marketplace, they could easily argue against a strategy based solely on clever communications. "We set up our principles to be the real deal," she said. "We knew we could not just tinker with our formulas. So we decided, let's start from scratch. Let's make sure we're renewable and recyclable, at least ninety-nine percent natural. Free of petrochemicals. Not tested on animals. Let's do it right."

They called it Green Works. They wanted Green Works to become a trusted adviser to mothers and fathers on how to care for a clean, green house.

What Changes in Technology Meant for Clorox

When the research scientists began putting together formulations for an all-natural household cleaner, most people in the company were skeptical that the group could create a formula as effective as a conventional cleaner. But when the tests came back from the labs and from consumers in their homes, the Clorox people knew they had themselves a blockbuster. Green Works performed as well as, or sometimes better than, normal cleaners.[10] Using technology and their scientific expertise, the researchers were able to transform natural ingredients into an effective cleaning product. The company was now prepared to compete in a world where the threat of shrinking natural resources created societal pressures for products that had a lesser impact.

This brand needed its own sense of character that was optimistic, forward thinking, and based solidly on the actual products. Buttimer's team chose the name Green Works because it was simple and offered efficacy as a primary benefit. Now it was time for a launch. To succeed, they relied on the twin tools of transparency and networks to support the launch. They used transparency to put their cards on the table and prove that the ingredients in Green Works were actually green. They used networks to power grassroots marketing to launch Green Works in the marketplace.

Clorox defied the cleaning product convention of leaving the ingredients off the label. It listed them, even though there was no regulatory requirement to do so. The marketers' biggest fear was being labeled as "greenwashers." They knew that their reputation as a bleach company meant they'd get extra scrutiny. Buttimer said, "We decided to put the Clorox name on the front label because we weren't hiding anything." The Green Works line was certified by the U.S. Environmental Protection Agency's Design for the Environment program.

Buttimer said that her team seeded the market with grassroots advertising: "We gave early product samples to bloggers, NGOs [nongovernmental organizations], media, to get feedback. We did that well before launch." The marketers gave special focus to shopper marketing; a major Earth Day initiative by Walmart gave the products special placement in the store through displays at the ends of aisles called *endcaps* and multibay displays called *fourways*. As a result, Green Works was placed in "action alley," the place where retailers put their hottest items.

What Changes in Human and Natural Resources Meant for Clorox

Based in Northern California and with a young workforce, Clorox turned out to be a natural place for employee engagement in sustainability. "Some of my proudest moments were when employees would come to me looking for opportunities to help out with the Green Works launch. As a result we have a team that is very passionate about what they're working on. I think that's absolutely a key variable in what has made us successful," said Buttimer.

"Like a lot of companies, we consider ourselves values-based. In the twenty-first century, that means being more sustainable," said Morrissey. "We're now building an eco-network where we invite employees who have a passion for this area to do something in addition to their day job. We've been blown away by the response. This has been incredibly successful as a means of engaging our employees, and that's another lens that we evaluate ourselves through."

With the launch of Green Works approaching, Clorox increased its stake in the sustainability sector by paying a premium price of over $900 million for Burt's Bees. Burt's Bees is a quirky company relentlessly committed to using only natural ingredients for its personal care products, which range from shampoo to lip balm. The Burt's Bees mission is "to make people's lives better every day naturally." The results of Clorox's ventures—repositioning Brita as a sustainability brand, launching Green Works, and buying Burt's Bees—have exceeded the company's plans and expectations. "Which," said Morrissey, "were quite high to start with." Each of the brands has experienced double-digit growth and is growing faster than the core brands in the company.

"It's no longer enough to be the best-performing product at the best price for the consumer; we also have to optimize in terms of sustainability what we put into the marketplace," said Morrissey. "We needed to own the fact that we're a consumer packaged-goods company making conventional cleaners, and as such, we have an exposure here. And we know that people are concerned about the toxics in the environment . . . There was a great deal of outreach to the stakeholder groups." Clorox knew that it wasn't credible enough on its own to launch a new green brand. It worked with the Environmental Protection Agency's Design for Environment Program (DfE) to have Green Works products reviewed before launch and validate the brand's green claims. The Green Works brand also partnered with the Sierra Club, making a donation to the organization and putting the group's logo on the bottle.

This was the first time the Sierra Club had ever partnered with a household cleaning product. Former Sierra Club executive director Carl Pope described the organization's decision to work with the Green Works brand as a way to popularize sustainable household products: "People are out there looking for solutions, and we [were] eager to give a giant kick-start to the market for green, affordable household cleaning products."[11] By getting the Sierra Club leadership engaged and genuinely supportive of the product, Clorox signaled to its audience of parents that the product was authentically green.

Which Changes in STaR Can You Exploit?

Time and again, changes in society, technology, and resources move sustainability to the desks of CEOs everywhere. By explicating, identifying, and analyzing the changes or trends that are affecting or could affect a business, you can begin mapping the key threats and opportunities on the STaR map. Table 2-1 presents an example of the opportunities in STaR mapping for Clorox. I use this framework throughout the book to explain why companies have infused sustainability into their core strategy. We'll start with defining the terms.

TABLE 2-1

Opportunities in STaR mapping: A Clorox example

	Questions to ask, assumptions to challenge	What to map	How change affects Clorox
Changes in society	• How do laws, preferences, and social morays of the society in which we function affect our business? • Are there changes coming that will affect how society responds to how our business performs? • Which opportunities might these changes provide our business? • Is our business a force that strengthens the societies in which we function, or weakens them?	• Regulatory environment • Customer preference • Trends in health and wealth • Supplier markets • The competition	• Growing customer demand for nontoxic cleaning products • Emerging chemical regulation in the European Union • New "green" competitors emerging on the horizon

| **Changes in technology** | • What are the opportunities for a radical increase in the productivity of our technology to make our work more efficient? What would it take to get there?
• How can technology protect us from erratic prices of energy?
• Do we have a consistent investment philosophy to ensure our technological leadership?
• Whom might we join with to create technological breakthroughs? | • Emerging production techniques
• Information availability
• Competitive differentiation
• Technological innovations
• Customer expectation | • Innovations allow non-petroleum-based cleaning products to have equal performance
• Transparency becomes a priority as information moves rapidly on the Internet |
| **Changes in resources** | • Which of our offerings are energy intensive to produce, to feed, or to transport?
• Which nonrenewable resources do we rely on for the business to function? What are the trends with these resources?
• What are the substitutes for these resources?
• What are the future trends in our labor markets?
• How will an aging population in industrialized countries affect us? | • Natural resource scarcity
• Energy price stability
• Waste disposal
• Supply-chain shocks
• Workforce development
• Talent recruiting
• Talent retention
• Diversity of talent pool | • Unstable petroleum prices suggest the need for alternatives
• Hazardous-waste disposal costs rising
• Employees want to work for a company that's perceived as a leader in sustainability |

Mapping Changes in Society

Society, the organization of human relationships that form the foundation on which your business functions, is more of a force, like gravity, than an object to be measured. Societies have four common characteristics:

1. A sense of place (real or virtual)

2. A common form of governance

3. A common language

4. Common culture (traditions and customs)

These characteristics enable trust within groups so that people can collaborate effectively to get what they need. This trust helps avoid conflicts and provides a rationale for meeting common social needs. Every business exists within the boundaries of different societies and is expected, just as you are, to take actions that strengthen these characteristics. If you pollute a river, you're destroying the society's sense of place. If you break laws wantonly, you're subtracting from the society's governance structures.

The ancient Greeks said that a society grows great when old men plant trees whose shade they know they will never sit in. A business relies on a healthy society in which you and others are planting trees for the future. Are you doing your share?

Mapping Changes in Technology

Technological advances are improving the quality of life for more people in more places than in any other time in history. Just look at the mother of all twentieth-century innovations: information technology. An old-fashioned copper wire can transmit twenty-four voice channels or about 1.5 megabytes of information per second. The much thinner and lighter optical fiber can transmit more than thirty-two thousand voice channels and more than 2.5 gigabytes of information per second.[12] By using these information channels, people who have been left out of the wealth creation of the twentieth century are beginning to be able to enter markets.

The Internet has connected people across the planet, improving access to information and people and increasing opportunities for invention and innovation. While it took thirteen years for TV to reach fifty million viewers, it took the Internet less than four years to reach the same number, and its influences are becoming ubiquitous. Today in coffeehouses across China, entrepreneurs are learning how to compete in the global economy. Children in mediocre urban schools can teach themselves programming languages and eventually enter the job market.

Other tools keep proliferating. There is now one cell phone for every two people in the world. That's 3.3 billion active cell phones in about twenty-five years, and according to Nokia, that number will grow to 5 billion by 2015, when two-thirds of the people on earth will have phones.[13] More than 1,000 cell phones are activated every minute, and these cell phones do far more than connect phone calls. Our parents could not have imagined that the largest camera manufacturer in the world is Nokia, not Kodak. An iPhone has more processing power than did the entire North American Air Defense command in 1965.

Slowly, this technology is spreading to the developing world. The Kenyan village of Muruguru has red dirt roads that are impassable in the rainy season. Most homes do not have electricity or indoor plumbing, and people mostly live a subsistence lifestyle. But recently, a cell-phone tower has arrived, and with it, modern information. One craftswoman uses her phone to call ahead and find out if her distant customers are in their villages. The calls save her hours of walking. Other townspeople use their phones to find the costs of coffee on the world market, to save them from unscrupulous middlemen. Columbia University economist Jeffrey Sachs has called for the global deployment of specially programmed cell phones to provide real-time data to health planners.[14] Residents of Muruguru can buy cell phones for about twenty dollars and airtime—in increments of just seventy-five cents in Kenya—which provides ten minutes of off-peak calling.[15]

For our purposes, we need to consider three characteristics of technology—that is, the use of knowledge and other tools to reduce the cost of completing tasks—in mapping how technological advances will change the external context.

1. Technology requires design. It starts with a need, moves to a set of specifications and ideation, and finishes with implementation and evaluation. Far too many companies

see new technology as an output rather than an input to their strategy.

2. Technology is value-dependent. Within the specifications, professionals judge or interpret the quality of products and services in terms of aesthetics, cost, environmental harm, and safety. What comes out of the pipe has a lot to do with what you put in. Garbage in, garbage out.

3. Technology shapes society as much as society innovates technology. By the nature of its design and intrinsic values, technology shapes society around it. Consider how the automobile enabled suburbs and otherwise changed how and where we live, or how the personal computer dispersed analytical and communications power and changed how we work and what we do.

Mapping Changes in Resources

I will say it again: The last great era of innovation was fueled by cheap energy. Over the last hundred years, we have been spending down the planet's stored energy that has come to us from the sun's rays over billions of years. We cannot keep using resources as though they are unlimited, yet many businesses continue to base their strategy and execution on this now invalid assumption.

For our purposes, *resources* include the natural or human assets needed to accomplish a task. They make society and technology work. Both human and natural resources are abundant, but limited. If we take care of those resources, we have enough human talent and natural capital to flourish. If we allow the poorest members of our society to suffer and our wealthiest members to abuse our natural resources, then the entire system on which we depend will fail, posing an existential problem to even the best-run business. Henry David Thoreau put it succinctly: "What is the use of a [fine] house if you have not got a tolerable planet to put it on?"[16]

The following facts about the degradation of the natural environment should inspire you to identify and map your company's opportunities to solve the natural resource problem through your product or service:

- We are cutting forests down. Every year, an area the size of the country of Panama disappears from the world's total forest area.[17] How and where can paper-intensive businesses innovate?

- We are burning through the last oil. Each day, we consume about 84 million barrels of oil, but produce only 83 million barrels of oil.[18] It's time to move beyond oil. Oil is a drain on the global economy, international security, and the climate. According to Amory Lovins, "those three reasons are good enough; we don't even need to talk about scarcity."[19] How will oil-dependant supply chains innovate?

- Our biodiversity is disappearing, wild fish are nearly extinct, and 90 percent of the large fish, like Chilean sea bass, monkfish, sturgeon, and swordfish—species that once thrived in our oceans—are nearly gone; scientists say that within forty years, all species of fish will fall below commercially viable levels.[20] When you include dry land, every day, 137 species across the planet go extinct, which is as much as one hundred times the natural rate of extinction. How will new businesses be built around the protection of our natural assets?

- Our climate is changing faster. Humanity releases about 30 billion tons of carbon dioxide a year into the atmosphere.[21] Which businesses will benefit from the natural limits of our atmosphere? Will carbon regulation speed the decline of aging business models?

- More consumers are coming. Five out of six people on the planet live at very low consumption rates. Most of the people alive right now are young. If China and India catch up to Western consumption rates with their current populations, then our aggregate resource usage will be that of nineteen billion people. Which businesses will be able to serve the needs of the coming middle class without swamping our natural systems?

Access to cheap resources, technological advances, and the process of globalization has conspired to benefit the developed world. Consider the following statistics:

- Almost every local environmental indicator in the United States has improved, from air quality to water quality, whereas air and water quality in developing countries like China are worsening.[22]

- The United States has defeated major diseases like polio, smallpox, diphtheria, and measles domestically.

- Some 70 percent of Americans own homes, compared with about 45 percent a century ago.[23]

- Life expectancy in the United States increased from 41 to 77 in the twentieth century. The global average life expectancy, however, is only 66 years. In countries like South Africa, Afghanistan, and Somalia, the average life expectancy remains below 50 years. In India, the twentieth century saw an increase in life expectancy from 30 to 69 years. And in Brazil and Vietnam, the life expectancy is 71 years.[24]

- Median incomes for African Americans are growing twice as fast as family median incomes as a whole. Yet in the United States and globally, incomes disparities grow. The median household income in South Africa is equivalent to US$22,600. The median income in Africa is still about US$1 a day.[25]

- Infant mortality in the United States is down 45 percent since 1980, compared with Bahrain, where infant and maternal mortality rates have been increasing.[26]

- In the United States in 1924, only 60 percent of fathers spent an hour a day with their kids; today, 83 percent do.[27]

- The average workweek in America declined from about sixty hours a week at the beginning of the twentieth century to less than forty a century later.[28]

- The average American had 1.8 hours of leisure activity per day in 1880, which had risen to 5.8 by the end of the millennium.[29]

- Of American homes, 95 percent are now centrally heated and 78 percent have air-conditioning.[30]

- Since 1993, the incidence of cancer has been going down in the United States, but is expected to double in Asia by 2020.[31]

In 1954, the inflation-adjusted price of a barrel of oil was $23.92.[32] At that time, M. King Hubbert, a geophysicist and former chief consultant of the General Geology, Exploration and Production Research Division of Shell Development Company, predicted that U.S. oil production would peak between 1965 and 1970.[33] It did in 1970.[34] An eloquent advertisement by oil firm Chevron sums it up well: "It took us 125 years to use the first trillion barrels of oil. We'll use the next trillion in 30. Energy will be one of the defining issues of this century. One thing is clear: the era of easy oil is over."[35]

The price of oil is higher now, but more important than its price is its volatility. In 2007–2008, the price of oil went from $47 a barrel to $147. For energy-intensive businesses, this rise was nothing short of a crisis. American Airlines reported that the cost of jet fuel per passenger to fly from Los Angeles to New York was $500, even as the airline was selling tickets for $390 to fill its seats.[36] Any business-critical resource that can triple in price within less than two years is too risky a dependence. And by the end of 2008, oil was again back under $50 a barrel. It's enough to make your head spin. Someday, we may pay $250 for a barrel of oil, or maybe not. No one knows. The only thing we can be sure of is that prices will be unpredictable. Consider the case of Dow Chemical Company.

In 2002, Dow spent $8 billion on petroleum-based products. At the peak of oil prices in 2008, Dow projected those costs to rise to

$32 billion a year.[37] These skyrocketing costs forced Dow to shuffle its strategy and raise its prices by 20 percent on all items energy intensive to produce, to feed, or to transport. As Dow CEO Andrew Liveris explained in a company statement, "The new level of hydrocarbons and energy costs is putting a strain on the entire value chain and is forcing difficult discussions with customers about resetting the value proposition for our products."[38] Dow sought strength in size by aggressively moving to purchase competitor Rohm & Haas at a premium price partially financed by a new partnership with the government of Kuwait. But then everything changed again. Prices quickly fell in the face of a global economic slowdown, and the Kuwaitis, no longer swimming in oil revenue, pulled out of the deal, leaving Dow high and dry. Businesses and governments that relied too heavily on oil with no easy substitutes vowed to act, yet again. Barack Obama, then presidential candidate, said, "The biggest problem with our energy policy has been to lurch from crisis to trance," and he committed to a sustained focus on renewable energy.[39]

Even in the 1950s, people knew that we could not rely on this cheap stored energy forever. In the same year that Swanson launched the TV dinner, scientists from Bell Laboratories created one of the first efficient solar cells by placing strips of silicon the size of razor blades in the sunlight. The strips captured electrons and converted them into electrical current.[40]

How Do You Identify and Prioritize Your Opportunities for Greater Sustainability?

The strategy for sustainability framework places a heavy focus on external awareness and internal capacity building in order to answer the questions, "Do you know what's happening?" and "Are you prepared to respond?" The purpose of the STaR map is to sense changes in the external world. Anticipating radical changes in society, technology, and resources, Maurice Levy, chairman and CEO of the global advertising holding firm Publicis Groupe, was early to begin retooling his communications group to address this new reality. For Levy, the need to be continuously aware and readily adapt was nothing new. In 1971, when he began working in the information technology department of the French firm Publicis, he introduced a magnetic tape system to back up the company's data. Shortly thereafter a fire destroyed everything, and thanks to Levy's magnetic tape, the data was saved and the company was up and running within a week.[41] Here are a few of the ways Levy is using a STaR map today. First, he noticed the rapid demographic changes in society and moved to acquire agencies in high-growth markets such as China, India, and Brazil. He identified promising new emerging technology—digital advertising—and bought Digitas for $1.3 billion, declaring that this sector would shortly account for 25 percent of his company's revenue. He also responded to resource changes by being the first advertising network to sign on to the United Nation's millennium development goals and creating a clearly articulated sustainability focus for his group.

You can build a STaR map for a product or for an entire business. If an enterprise is heavily resource dependent, it will want to spend more time drilling down exactly how it will see those resources' availabilities changing. If the business is more service oriented, it will want to spend more time looking at how changes in society and technology will move the business landscape.

Now that you know what you'll be mapping, how will you go about mapping it? Most companies split their insight research between (1) reading everything they can, (2) investigating changes with their own eyes, and (3) talking to outsiders to get different views. The entire mapping process could last a few hours or a few weeks, but rarely does it last longer than a month. Your task is to get a snapshot of the world outside your doors.

The astonishing rate at which we have seen change take place in the last part of the twentieth century will accelerate into the twenty-first century.[42] The STaR changes themselves are largely out of our control (see, for example, "Viewing Climate Change as an Opportunity to Innovate"). How we anticipate and navigate these shifts will determine twenty-first-century business winners and losers, just as they did for Swanson & Sons in the 1950s.

Viewing Climate Change as an Opportunity to Innovate

WHEN GARRETT HARDIN WROTE "The Tragedy of the Commons" to chronicle the threat to resources that everyone could use but that no one owned, he could not have imagined that the earth's atmosphere would soon become a commons under siege.[a] The idea of the commons originated in medieval Europe, where villages of herders relied on shared pastureland to graze their livestock. Because no one individual was made responsible for maintaining the land, it was at risk of overgrazing. If any individual chose to use more than a proper share of the pasture, everyone would suffer.

These trends have brought us to where we are now, staring into the specter of climate change. Climate change, or global warming, describes the warming of the planet because of excessive levels of greenhouse gases in the atmosphere. I use the term *climate change* instead of *global warming* because sometimes, in some places, the weather will get colder, or more intense, or just plain strange.

The chief driver of climate change is the buildup of carbon dioxide (CO_2) in the atmosphere. There is nothing inherently unnatural about carbon dioxide; it harms nothing until amassed in large quantities in the atmosphere. But burning fossil fuels and burning the great tropical rain forests of the Amazon, the Congo, and Indonesia—forests that have stored billions of tons of CO_2 for millennia—have spiked atmospheric carbon far above what it should be to maintain the fragile ecosystem of the earth. Let's look at the breakdown of greenhouse gas emissions:[b]

- Of all CO_2 emissions, 59 percent comes largely from energy, transportation, and industrial processes.

Power production is our number one emitter, with coal being the biggest culprit.

- Another 17 percent represents the cutting of forests. Since trees are a natural mechanism for sequestering CO_2, their elimination hampers the natural absorption of this gas. Here's the place to start: by addressing this environmental problem, we address countless social, cultural, and economic factors as well. Stopping defor- estation in tropical areas means protecting the richest biodiversity on the planet and improving the quality of life for the people who live in the forest. Places like Brazil, Papua New Guinea, Indonesia, and the Congo could be completely transformed for the better if the rampant cutting were stopped and if new ways to reduce poverty in those nations were funded. The single cheapest way we can slow global warming is by protecting the last great rain forests on the planet.

- Another 14 percent of greenhouse gas emissions comes from agriculture, which produces high levels of CH_4, or methane, largely from livestock. Methane production is a tougher problem to tackle, because most of the potential solutions involve deep lifestyle changes, like changing your diet to eat little or no meat. Waste disposal and energy production also pro- duce small amounts of methane, which is 20 to 25 times more potent as a greenhouse gas than CO_2.

- The remaining 9 percent is driven by various other processes that emit nitrous oxide and fluorinated gases—the so-called "High Global Warming Potential" gases including HFCs, PFCs, and SF6.[c] Nitrous oxide also comes largely from agriculture, while fluorinated gases—at about 1 percent of the total—are the result of various industrial processes, such as the use of HFCs (hydrofluorocarbons) in refrigerators and air conditioners.

Ironically, these HFCs were born of the solution to another problem. In 1989, the world agreed to the Montreal Protocol, which succeeded in banning chlorofluorocarbons (CFCs) from items like refrigerants and aerosols. These CFCs were depleting the ozone layer, which protects the earth from the dangerous rays of the sun. The destruction of the ozone layer has increased skin cancer in humans and has had countless effects on other species. But depleting the ozone layer is different from climate change, which refers to long-term changes in the earth's weather.

But here's the catch: HFCs are many times more potent than CO_2 molecules at contributing to climate change. By solving one problem—the depletion of the ozone layer—we contributed to another problem: global warming through HFCs. If it sounds as though tinkering with the planet's ecosystems is complicated, it is.

The results of climate change include melting ice caps and higher sea levels, changes in temperature (both up and down), and an increase in irregular weather events such as hurricanes. Glaciers will retreat, new diseases will proliferate, agriculture yields will shift, species will go extinct, and mosquitoes will increase their range. Basically, all the bad things that befell the pharaohs in Egypt will strike the planet in our lifetimes, unless we decarbonize our economy.[d] Hunter Lovins, cofounder of Rocky Mountain Institute in Snowmass, Colorado, has called it "global weirding" because your environment—the weather, the bugs, the animals, the crops—will just differ from when you were a kid.

Climate change will increase costs as energy is taxed, or "capped," and permits are auctioned to control the amount carbon is released into the atmosphere. This capping has already placed a value on carbon of about ten dollars per ton of CO_2, but it will mostly likely trade between thirty and one hundred dollars per ton released within a few years.[e]

By 2020, we must reduce the amount of CO_2 released by 50 percent below 1990 levels, since 1990 is used as the baseline year for most global carbon calculations. Since billions of people on the planet still must access reliable energy—and since most of the CO_2 being released comes from the industrialized world—as much as 90 percent of this decrease should come from those of us who have experienced the benefits of the "free sky" era. The free-sky era is over; from now on, we'll have to pay for the right to put pollution in the sky, just as we have to pay someone to take away our garbage or our sewage.

a. Garrett Hardin, "The Tragedy of the Commons," *Science* 162, no. 3859 (13 December 1968): 1243–1248.

b. U.S. Environmental Protection Agency, "Methane," 19 October 2006, www.epa.gov/methane/scientific.html, gives methane a CO_2 equivalent rating of 21. National Oceanic and Atmospheric Administration, "Greenhouse Gases, Carbon Dioxide And Methane, Rise Sharply in 2007," *Science Daily*, 24 April 2008, www.sciencedaily.com/releases/2008/04/080423181652.htm, gives methane a CO_2 equivalent rating of 25.

c. http://www.epa.gov/highgwp/sources.html.

d. Intergovernmental Panel on Climate Change, "Climate Change 2007: Synthesis Report," Intergovernmental Panel on Climate Change Plenary 27, Valencia, Spain, 12–17 November 2007, 36, www.ipcc.ch/pdf/assessment-report/ar4/syr/ar4_syr.pdf.

e. A *cap and trade* is a system that allows a government or an international body to set a limit (cap) on a certain type of pollution. The organization then issues permits—also called allowances—that polluters must purchase to cover all the pollution they release. Sources with extra permits can sell or trade them to other sources, thereby allowing them to cover emissions beyond their individual cap.

Act Now: Putting STaR to Work

You can employ a STaR map at many levels of your business interactions. Here are some specific ways you can gain insight through STaR mapping:

- Just as all politics is local, so is strategy implementation. How are changes in society, technology, and resources affecting you as an employee, a manager, an entrepreneur, a student, or a job-seeker?

- Draft a STaR map for your career. How will changes in society affect your career? What relationships can you develop to prepare for those changes? What are the new technologies that leaders will adopt in your job? How can you be the first to adopt those tools? What resource changes will affect you directly? Can you develop substitutes?

- Create a monthly STaR update that you share with your leadership team. Include articles or lists of major events that are changing the external context. It can be brief; the purpose is to align your team to the same story about where the world is heading so the team manages accordingly.

- Spend a day with your most important customer. What is your customer worried about? How is this company or person planning for context changes? Do you both have the same story about what's going to happen next?

CHAPTER THREE

Setting Your North Star and Initiating the TEN Cycle

The Tools of Implementation

WHEN I FIRST STARTED working with retailers, I needed to understand one of the modern human's natural habitats—the supermarket. What do people actually do there? Do they choose name brands instead of private-label brands? Do they buy organic? Do they buy everything from one store, or do they shop from many?[1] Why does the average American mom spend about an hour a day shopping?[2]

So I started spending time every week in stores. To my surprise, the people I observed were leaving happy, usually with wide smiles. They were excited to get home and tear into a package of Lay's potato chips, or make a home-cooked lasagna, or drink a well-deserved beer at the end of a long day.[3] In the produce department,

I watched browsers pick up arugula, inspect it, and wonder what it was. In the liquor section, one man must have mistaken me for an employee: "Which wine does not taste too much like vinegar?" "Yellow Tail," I blurted out, surprised and probably violating every "secret shopper" ethical code. "Yellow Tail is an affordable and drinkable New Zealand white wine."

At one store, I watched a father with an infant strapped to his chest in a Baby Bjorn carrier trying to control his two other children. The older one was recklessly pushing his younger sibling around in the shopping cart. When the dad yelled at his eldest, his baby started wailing. Nearby, his wife was reading the labels of Soft-Soap hand soap and Suave shampoo, both value brands.[4] When the father finally calmed the three kids down, he joined his wife in her inspection of labels.

"Which do you think we can water down?" he asked. They had agreed that they could save money by adding water to their household cleaners and were trying to decide which one was more dilutable. After talking about it for a few minutes and calming one more fight between the two older children, they finally decided that they could water down the Soft-Soap but that they probably could not water down Suave.

Your Sustainability Efforts Must Serve Core Needs

These parents were not looking for an organic shampoo; they needed something that could save them money—and sustainability-driven innovation can do that by compacting soaps, reducing packages, and decreasing the need for hot water. When Walmart asked its manufacturers to look at their goods through the lens of sustainability, one manufacturer of baby car seats focused on packaging. The company's North Star goal was to ensure the safety of as many babies as possible, and so it wanted to get more seats into the hands of customers.

For years, it had shipped its seats in large, white boxes for protection. If it replaced this big, white box with clear, durable plastic wrap, Walmart could fit more car seats in the trucks, cutting down on fuel costs. Since the package was smaller, the store could stock more seats on the floor, which kept the item in stock and in easy view. As soon as the company changed its packaging, sales of seats increased as well.[5]

Unfortunately, companies that have jumped onto the sustainability bandwagon too often develop and position their innovations as luxury goods at premium prices, appealing primarily to wealthier consumers. For example, I'm sure that the organic cotton sheets described in an online "green-living" catalog as "Lucia jacquard bedding . . . free of harsh chemical softeners or chlorine" are lovely. They might be comfortable, but the larger challenge is to construct sustainable products that match the core needs of a much larger segment of society than the people who can afford $740 for a queen-size set of those Portuguese bedsheets.[6]

So how do you find out what people really want? Just watch what happens when people run out of money in the checkout line, a situation that happens for all sorts of reasons, and even more so in an economic downturn. In the last decade, about 40 percent of American workers have lived paycheck to paycheck.[7] Globally, some three billion people live on less than three dollars a day, and because they have less credit, smaller pantries, and few options for savings, they tend to shop more often.[8] In the United States, some people never had, or no longer have, credit cards. Other people set a strict budget and stop spending when they reach it. What they keep and what they put back reveals their priorities, however simplistically and unscientifically. In a supermarket in Montana over about an hour, I saw two shoppers run out of money during the checkout process. Shopper 1 immediately abandoned cheese and eggs and kept the chips, cookies, and soda. Shopper 2 ditched the vegetables first. Almost every time I see people hit their pocketbook's limit at the cashier, they remove the healthier items. Maybe the healthier alternative costs more. Or maybe they do not consider the healthier alternative a necessity. Or maybe, when strapped for cash, they find enjoyment in the more decadent choices.[9]

Watching people shop always reminds me that a strategy for sustainability provides an opportunity to get closer to customers—by saving them money if that is their priority. Or by improving their health and well-being. Or by surprising them pleasantly with innovations that you created by networking with other companies. Or by giving your salespeople a goal that they can believe in enough to share with customers. Or by providing a product label that would have helped the aforementioned parents with the three cranky kids make the more sustainable trade-off—and save them money.

North Star Goals: Guiding Decisions and Actions

In some aspects, running a company is not all that different from sustaining a busy, three-child family. The parents are struggling to pay the mortgage while striving to put away money for a college education, all the while dealing with tantrums and illnesses and unforeseen events. Companies need to take care of their three constituencies, too—customers, employees, and suppliers—constantly innovating on the core product or service, investing in sales and marketing, and finding new ways to save costs in the supply chain. For most families, the North Star is clear—provide the kids more opportunities than what they had. For companies, finding a North Star can be trickier. See "Setting Your North Star Goal" for some specific techniques you can use and questions you can ask yourself and your coworkers to narrow down your company's goals.

Skiers report snow blindness when the sun reflects off the snow and obscures their vision. Is there also "green blindness" that affects companies trying to take a leadership stance? Something happens when the word *sustainability* comes up. People forget the business. They become fixated on the environmental aspects of sustainability and forget about the economics. Hoards of midlevel managers flock to corporate social responsibility [CSR] conferences to empathize with each other about how difficult it is to get staff, resources, and management attention. The most common question I hear in these meetings is, "How did you get management to listen?"

If the goal were to build an information technology system, senior people across the organization would certainly come together to get management attention, time, and resources. Similarly, small, rebel factions across the organization would never have to work across department lines to "build the business case." Quite the opposite; without the business case, there would be no discussion. Why, then, do people struggle with implementing sustainability efforts?

They get stuck trying to be good corporate citizens and currying favor with outsiders, never actually figuring out how to connect sustainability to their core business. Some people almost feel guilty talking about sustainability as a business driver. But that's exactly the approach that would allow them to make the biggest change in the world.

Their sustainability initiative must be core to the business—bold, not bolted on, not "feel good once a year" for employees. *Economist* editor Daniel Franklin explains this point: "Many companies pretend that their sustainability strategy runs deeper than it really does. It has become almost obligatory for executives to claim that CSR is 'connected to the core' of corporate strategy, or that it has become 'part of the DNA.' In truth, even ardent advocates of sustainability struggle to identify more than a handful of examples. More often the activities that go under the sustainability banner are a hotchpotch of pet projects at best tenuously related to the core business."[10] To be successful, you need to peel off the green blinders and start thinking of sustainability as a new tool set, like information technology or globalization, that can help you reinvigorate a business.

At this point, you should have a clearer view of the situation facing a business, relative to changes in society, technology, and resources, based on your STaR map for the organization. Now a company needs to develop North Star goals to guide the whole organization toward executing a strategy for sustainability. Remember, a North Star goal is an overarching business goal that has these characteristics:

- It is optimistic and aspirational.

- Your organization can achieve it in five to fifteen years.

- It applies across the enterprise.

- Every employee can personally act on it.

- It connects to the core of your business.

- It drives excitement and passion in your organization.

- It serves a higher purpose than business profitability.

- It solves a great human challenge.

- It leverages your organization's strengths.

Smaller companies founded more recently, like Stonyfield Farm and method, were founded with their North Star goals in mind. Their North Star goal connected solving a great human challenge with their organizational strengths. The founders knew the global human challenges that the companies hoped to solve. They built the core of their business around a higher purpose that inevitably drives excitement and passion in the organization. Many older companies, like Johnson & Johnson, have organizational beliefs that point them toward their North Star. Johnson & Johnson's credo begins, "We believe that our first responsibility is to the doctors, nurses and patients, to mothers and fathers and all others who use our products and services.[11] JCPenney was founded on the Golden Rule as its operating belief.[12] These strong, credo-based companies can move quite quickly into a strategy for sustainability, since tying the business functions even more closely to solving global human challenges is something the companies already desire. For other companies not built with sustainability in mind, there are a few types of North Star goals that they adopt:

- Internal organizing or operating goals

- Game-changing goals

- Product- or service-changing goals

Internal organizing North Star goals help provide a level of specificity and clarity to the organization. In 2008, for example, Hilton created four initiatives for its hotels around the world: (1) reduce the energy consumption of direct operations by 20 percent, (2) reduce CO_2 emissions by 20 percent, (3) reduce waste output by 20 percent, and (4) reduce water consumption by 10 percent.[13] These goals represent millions of dollars of cost savings for Hilton and require everyone, from the housekeepers to the operating engineers, to lend a hand. In 2007, Procter & Gamble set a five-year goal to "sell $20 billion worth of 'sustainable innovation products'; reduce carbon dioxide emissions, energy use, water use and waste by 10 percent and deliver 2 billion liters of clean water to children around the world." For P&G, leveraging its global reach to push $20 billion of new "sustainable innovation products" is a way to engage every person in the P&G organization.[14] Sales is what they do.

If you set an internal transformation goal (like Hilton's), then first look at the major resources used in your business and then project the efficiencies you could achieve through different scales of effort. Most companies can exceed even their most ambitious efficiency and waste-reduction goals, because they have much waste in their systems. Without a major conservation effort, from 1975 to 2006, the United States made a dollar of real gross domestic product with 48 percent less total energy, 54 percent less oil, 64 percent less directly used natural gas, 17 percent less electricity, and two-thirds less water.[15] Goals for reducing the absolute amount of CO_2 are harder to hit, particularly if yours is a growing business. Do not let that dissuade you. Once you have measured your carbon footprint, your first step should be to increase efficiency, which will result in increasing the profit per unit of carbon consumed. Walter Stahel, who defined the cradle-to-cradle concept, recommends using the metric of dollars of profit per unit of material consumed.[16] Either way, goals to reduce absolute resource consumption are critical across the economy.

Game-changing North Star goals change the frame of the external environment so that it will benefit the world and your business. InterfaceFLOR, based in Atlanta, is the world's largest modular floor coverings manufacturer. It has set out "to be the first company that, by its deeds, shows the entire industrial world what sustainability is in all its dimensions: People, process, product, place and profits—by 2020—and in doing so we will become restorative through the power of influence." Not only has this mission diverted over one hundred million pounds of material from the landfill, the company has calculated that it avoided $372 million in cumulative waste cost from 1995 to 2007.[17] Under the leadership of its CEO Kevin Roberts, Saatchi & Saatchi has set out to "help a billion people create their own personal sustainability practices through the products and people that touch their lives."[18] He believes that every company will soon be setting North Star goals for itself. "The brands of the future," he says, "will each have a purpose and that priceless competitive advantage which comes from doing the right thing when no one is looking."[19]

Product- or service-changing North Star goals inject sustainability innovations into a company's portfolio of brands. In the *leadership-brands model*, a company, like Clorox, analyzes society's changing needs, identifies technologies or brand attributes that help the company meet those needs, and then buys or starts a brand that is separate from its core brand equity and that reaches out to the "sustainable" consumer base. Companies typically also attempt to use the experience of these leadership brands to improve their core company. Burt's Bees is a learning laboratory for Clorox. Board members from Ben & Jerry's, which was purchased by Unilever, advise their corporate parent; gadfly businessman Gary Hirshberg's Stonyfield Farm is determined to aid its new parent,

Groupe Danone; and L'Oreal bought The Body Shop in part to bring a new consciousness to the company.

Typically, although not exclusively, leadership brands command a price premium over existing brands and are a means of growing revenue. Take ice cream, for example. When it bought Ben & Jerry's, Unilever already had brands like Klondike and Breyers. Ben & Jerry's gave it a means, through premium organic ice cream, to put a higher-priced product on the market.

Some companies fear the risk involved in this model. They worry that consumers will ask why their mainstream brands are not sustainable as well. If organic is important, why sell products that use pesticides? Some companies, like General Mills, do not make organic versions of their core products, like Cheerios.[20] Kellogg, on the other hand, has experimented with organic versions of its products, like Raisin Bran. It's a dynamic moment, and the rules are just now being written. For Clorox, the company had refined its target audience as the mom who was looking for a brand that was optimistically forward-thinking. "We didn't think she'd find a brand extension believable," said Jessica Buttimer. "She was looking for a trusted adviser, and we wanted to give her one."

In the *integrating-innovations model*, a company slowly improves the products it has without making a big fuss or suggesting that making a product sustainable is anything out of the ordinary. Brands have always improved their products to match the times. Integrating innovation is often a model for building customer loyalty by following changing consumer trends, increasing convenience, or reducing the cost of using the product.

One example of a company that is integrating innovations is Procter & Gamble. P&G released Tide Coldwater, a formulation of its best-selling laundry detergent, Tide, that allowed consumers to have the same cleaning results when using cold water. It was marketed as a way for consumers to hold on to their money by saving 80 percent of the energy normally required for each load of hot-water laundry.[21] The company didn't make a big deal about the fact that if every American changed to cold-water laundry, it would go a long way toward reaching the CO_2 reduction commitment that the U.S. negotiators made (although never ratified by the Senate) in the Kyoto Protocol, the first global compact on climate change. For Procter & Gamble, the decision to integrate sustainability innovations into its core brands was a natural choice. At the heart of the worldview of Procter & Gamble is the belief that the consumer is boss. Founded in 1837 by combining the businesses of William Procter, a candle maker, and James Gamble, a soap maker, P&G is now one of the largest companies on the planet, with over three billion transactions a day. Its portfolio includes Tide detergent, Pringles potato chips, Duracell batteries, and Bounty paper towels.

Len Sauers is the vice president of global sustainability and helms Procter & Gamble's sustainability initiative, although it's frustratingly difficult to get him to explain his specific role in its innovation cycle, since he says without a hint of sarcasm, "There's no *I* in P&G." P&G has chosen to integrate sustainability innovations into its core products instead of creating a set of smaller product lines that target the deep-green consumer. "As a company, we believe we can make the most meaningful difference by targeting the mainstream consumer, and that means we need to give her a product with no tradeoffs whatsoever," he said. "We believe our products should have the best of environmental sustainability as well as meeting needs for performance and value."[22]

To determine where it could make the biggest impact on environmental sustainability, P&G conducted a life-cycle analysis of the energy use of its products. It found that across the entire company, the largest use of energy was in the consumer-use phase of laundering and that value was driven by the heating of water for the laundry cycle. "This surprised me," Sauers said. "I thought our highest energy impact was going to be somewhere in the manufacturing process."

With this fact in hand, Sauers approached the head of R&D. He said, "It was clear to me that if you wanted to make a meaningful difference, targeting this metric of energy was the right thing to do, enabling consumers to wash in cold water was the key." The head of

Company product energy usage from life cycle perspective

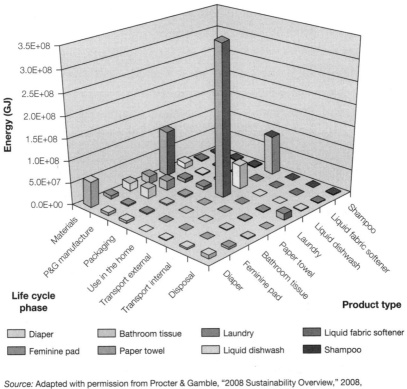

Source: Adapted with permission from Procter & Gamble, "2008 Sustainability Overview," 2008, www.pg.com/innovatingsustainability/innovating/managing.shtml.

R&D understood the opportunity immediately and set the scientists to work, while the products research group began to gather consumer insights to decide how to commercialize the idea. "The challenge was that the consumer will not accept trade-offs," said Sauer. "She wants performance in cold water that was the same in hot water."[23]

P&G's scientists began to tackle the challenge. They started with the problem: soiled clothes. Soil is hydrophobic, meaning it repels water. Detergents work by using surfactants to get water into the dirt or grime on a piece of clothing to loosen it. Surfactants have the ability to bridge hydrophobic and hydrophilic (water-attracting) molecules. So a surfactant helps brings the water into the soil. To make Tide clean just as well in cold water as it does in hot water, the researchers needed to replace the traditional anionic surfactant with a highly soluble alkyl sulfate (HSAS). An HSAS is more soluble than traditional surfactants, so it gets into solution better in cold water. Voilà, a cold-water detergent offered the consumer the same cleaning performance that hot water could. P&G's scientists are constantly looking for materials that are more soluble in cold water than the present surfactants, but the life-cycle analysis, the process of making P&G's energy effects transparent, provided the opportunity to create a commercial breakthrough.

This is the type of innovation that can come from looking at a challenge through the lens of sustainability. Said Sauers, "We do see sustainability as an opportunity. Consumers are becoming more and more eco-aware. If you're able to give them sustainability in a way that doesn't require them to make a trade-off, it's a huge business opportunity."

Setting Your North Star Goal

EVERYONE ALWAYS ASKS how to go about setting a North Star goal. Well, you're in for some fun. Start by taking your planning group out on a trip for some creative stimuli and to see what other companies are doing to innovate. We like to take companies from the food world on sustainability bike tours of San Francisco, stopping to see a successful local bakery called Mission Pie, where at-risk kids make delicious organic pies. We take them to the Ferry Plaza farmer's market, to see how local growers are experimenting with heirloom seeds and new growing techniques. We visit a supermarket and, looking at the cars in the lot, try to guess who's shopping inside. And we talk to people at Dolores Park and Atlas Café and just watch what they're eating and drinking and reading. Having a day with some common experiences and references helps align a planning group.[a]

A caution: do not get too caught up in endless competitive analysis, since the field of sustainability as it applies to business is in its infancy. Most of your competitors have not really begun or are in the "green" phase of their development, meaning that they are cleaning up their manufacturing, distribution, and production of certain brands or operations. Nonetheless, using the commonly understood framework of a SWOT analysis—strengths, weaknesses, opportunities, and threats—is a safe tool for helping you establish an agreed-on reference point describing where your company sits today. When using SWOT, insert the categories of sustainability—social, economic, environmental, and cultural—to jog your thinking about how these four categories interact with traditional business metrics.

Once you've got this common reference point, ask each member of your planning team to take fifteen minutes to write newspaper headlines that would affect your business some fifteen years into the future. Discuss the headlines, and prioritize them by what you think is most realistic and most actionable. Then ask the group to write down North Star goals that answer the challenges of those headlines. Is there more turbulence or less turbulence in the future you see? Is your company still around? Do you aspire to have an affect on the future headlines? Or is your dream to be on the shores of a Caribbean island? What would need to change now to make the future headlines more positive? Will the world be better or worse in fifteen years? As you ask these questions, start collecting ideas for what your North Star goals are, always keeping in mind that the goals need to be core to the business, engaging to your team, and connected to a higher purpose for the rest of the world.

Frequently, companies start on their way to their North Star by creating a separate sustainability leadership brand. A North Star goal might be, "Launch a new line of low-cost, naturally derived, zero-waste widgets that become 30 percent of our revenue in three years and inspires every other product in our category to follow in five years." If you go this route, here are the questions you should consider:

- Will you give this brand the freedom to innovate on ingredients, packaging, and distribution?

- Is a visionary brand leader running the effort? Does this person have a winning track record with business innovations?

- How will you integrate and celebrate the lessons from this brand into my mainstream products teams?

If you're considering integrating innovations, here are the questions you should consider:

- How will you communicate to consumers and to the company that these innovations are happening?

- How do you measure the success of the investments in these innovations?

- How do you keep the momentum going when you are not necessarily receiving consumer feedback for these innovations?

Finally, ask yourself and your team members these questions about your goal (or goals):

- How optimistic and aspirational is it, compared with employees' typical performance goals?

- Can your organization achieve it in five to fifteen years? Which variables affect your time horizon?

- Does the goal apply across the enterprise? If not, then which operation or process is missing? Why?

- Can every employee contribute to achieving it as a core part of his or her job, and can you offer long-term incentives for each person?

- How does it connect to the core of your business? What is the business model?

- Does it drive excitement and passion in your organization? You'll know that it has when you lose some control over the effort because it's being seized by employees.

- Which purpose higher than business profitability does it serve?

- Which great human challenge does it help to solve? Who else is solving that?

- How does it leverage your organization's strengths? Which strengths in particular will factor into your success?

a. I'm a big fan of bike tours. The staff at Saatchi & Saatchi S have taken on biking as a major cultural aspect of our company and came up with the idea of bike trips for clients. (The S stands for sustainability, but since we're part of Saatchi, we just use the S, because Saatchi & Saatchi believes that all good brands should be surrounded with mystery, sensuality, and intimacy.) The first few times we did this, we had some hiccups, placing novice bikers on the hills of San Francisco on our beat-up loaner bikes that we have around the office. In case you're going to do this, make sure you take the time to check everyone's physical conditioning and make sure that the rider's bike is fitted and functional. Safety first.

A Model for Execution: Transparency, Engagement, and Network

Why do the best-laid plans often go astray? As I have said, the ongoing use of short-term metrics guarantees a focus on short-term profitability. The time frame of the metrics must change, and North Star goals inherently call for a five- to fifteen-year horizon. The core of a strategy for sustainability is your desire and commitment to create an organization—or a business unit, or a product or service, or even a process—that will endure long after you are gone. It will be your leadership legacy, regardless of your job title at your organization.

Other corporate killjoys to sustainability include problems related to the TEN cycle (the positive-feedback loop of transparency, engagement, and networking):

- *Poor communications*—In such times of change, communications must be top-notch both internally and externally, not just to keep everyone informed but also to move toward greater transparency as an organization.

- *Managerial complacency*—Equally important, a movement without "fire in the belly" will slide into mediocrity and die a slow death. Companies with a strong sense of action and urgency can continually implement change and stave off complacency, even as they experience success.

- *Executive hypocrisy*—If leaders fail to walk the talk, then no one else will. Whether it is executives taking large bonuses while employees take cuts in health-care benefits or stocking disposable cups at the coffee station while advocating for a green building, the message comes across clear.

- *Corporate isolation*—The internal disconnect is generally mirrored in a broader disconnection from society, as evidenced by such gaffes as executives flying on corporate jets while begging for bailout money. Corporate isolation results in a company being battered by financial and social trends rather than its being prepared to respond to them.

- *Staff apathy*—The final and most common systemic failure is a disengaged staff. Sustainability simply cannot be achieved without engaged employees.

Companies that incorporate sustainability into their core business strategy have figured out that to achieve sustainability, they must create an organization prepared for adaptation and growth. *Organizational qualities are far more important than any absolute goal.* In my experience and borrowing from nature's simple rules, I have found that the TEN cycle in particular—transparency of information and communications (nature is transparent), engagement of managers and employees at all levels (nature works systemically), and a growing network of sustainability partners (nature forms groups)—makes for a sustainable organization.

Each of these qualities enables the organization to see the outside situation clearly and adjust its behavior accordingly. All three work in a cycle, rather like pulmonary respiration, where several exchanges occur rapidly and cyclically, so as to maintain the being. Now let's explore two examples of putting the TEN cycle into action.

New Businesses: Founded on a North Star Goal for Sustainability

Look at Stonyfield Farm, a fast-growing dairy producer of organic products like yogurt. It is successfully converting its North Star goal—to move organic products from a niche market to the mainstream, so as to improve the physical health of people and the planet—into a TEN cycle of actions toward greater transparency, fuller employee engagement, and a stronger sustainability network.

Gary Hirshberg, the company's "CE-YO" (YO = yogurt), has been an organic since the 1970s. Along with Samuel Kaymaen, Hirshberg founded Stonyfield Farm on a farm in Wilton, New Hampshire, in the 1980s as an organic farming school. Warm and earnest, Hirshberg seems as comfortable in a barn as in a boardroom and floats between both with ease. Stonyfield Farm's North Star goal, bringing organic to the mainstream, has been at its core since its founding. Hirshberg and Kaymaen started their yogurt business with a few Jersey cows and a great-tasting yogurt recipe. They milked the cows and made the yogurt themselves, passionately believing that their little farm effort could make a difference.

Today, Stonyfield Farm does over $300 million in sales annually and is the third-largest yogurt brand in the United States.[24] "I'm very proud of the organic industry's progress in becoming a $20 billion sector of the U.S. food economy and of our decade-long plus-20 percent compounded annual growth rate (CAGR). But organic is still only 3.6 percent of U.S. food—we're a rounding error," Hirshberg said.[25]

Once a company has a North Star goal, it begins to work on the organizational capacity to implement that goal. For Stonyfield Farm, one aspect of its sustainability strategy is to constantly increase its energy efficiency as a means of reducing costs to keep prices down.

Step 1: Increase Information Transparency

The first step for Stonyfield Farm was to open up information to the organization. Yogurt making is an energy-intense endeavor, with high costs in the transportation, production, and refrigeration of the product.

Employees at Stonyfield Farm held information sessions about climate change, and they are familiar about how it threatens both the planet and their business. The cows they rely on for their product have a large carbon footprint.

Step 2: Engage Employees

To engage its employees, Stonyfield Farm set up interdisciplinary "Mission-Action-Program" teams (MAP teams), each team with a goal to improve the company's climate performance. The transportation MAP team, for instance, wanted to reduce its carbon footprint and mapped its entire route system, looking at which routes have loads that are less than full. The team called these LTTs, or less-than-truckloads, and focused its effort directly on them. The transportation MAP team was able to achieve a 50 percent reduction in its carbon footprint in the first eighteen months.

Hirshberg believes that getting midlevel employees involved was critical. "I think we all have to remember that all change starts at the edges. But it only becomes permanent when it makes it into the middle," he said. "Life on the edge among the change agents is very stimulating. We need to remember that we haven't succeeded until these new practices become widely adopted by managers and employees and a normal part of "business as usual.""

Sometimes, the changes were as easy as learning how to turn. The transportation MAP team asked the yogurt drivers to make fewer left turns when possible, which the team had learned from UPS as a way to save energy. Waiting for lights or for traffic to pass can consume more fuel than stringing a couple right turns together.[26] The drivers also reduced idling time. They installed on the trucks a backup power system that allowed the refrigerator units to work without the truck engine's burning fuel.

Step 3: Engage the Network

The role of a leader like Hirshberg is to encourage employees to look outside the company for a solution. Adopting the UPS idea for fewer left turns saved Stonyfield Farm money and cost nothing to develop. Engaging customers is a critical part of using the network because it guarantees that the idea is connected to the core of your business. Without customers, there is no business. "We worked with our customer service team to talk this through with the customer," Hirshberg said. "The customer service people would say, 'That's only seven pallets—if you do three more, it will save you on next week's shipments.'"

Customer service agents offered better terms for customers who helped them get the trucks full. More controversially, Stonyfield Farm began to negotiate deals with other perishable-food companies to share truck space. This goes against the hard-edged competition in the food business, wherein your distribution system is a core part of your competitive advantage. But when the company evaluated the idea against the four aspects of sustainability—social, economic, environmental, and cultural—the choice was clear. Collaborating with its competitors produced societal benefits by keeping prices down, saved money for Stonyfield, reduced the amount of carbon going into the atmosphere, and supported a great number of local farmers. In essence, Stonyfield Farm employed the TEN cycle to implement sustainability (table 3-1).

"The layperson might get bored," Hirshberg said. "But for us, this is totally exciting stuff that just simply works. Oh yeah, and those efforts generated $2.5 million in savings last year." Everyone at the company knew that the transportation MAP team helped everyone make his or her bonus at the end of the year. "We encouraged people to get started, and then they kept asking the question, why not?" Hirshberg said.

Hirshberg is not concerned about his competitors' jumping on the organic bandwagon now. "The problem with the club that we had was that it was a very small club," he said.

"Some people say that the organic movement is peaking," he added. "If we're only dependent on selling ethics and virtues and moral righteousness, then we deserve to have peaked. We need to be genuinely meaningful to 60 percent of the people and not just the club that knows all the lingo. It's terribly myopic. More importantly, it's boring."

TABLE 3-1

Stonyfield Farm's use of the TEN cycle to save gas

Transparency	Engagement	Network
Shared with customers and employees the data about the costs of unfilled trucks	Empowered its employees to create MAP teams that engaged customers and competitors in a solution	Networked with other perishable-food companies to fill up the unused space in their trucks; provided discounts to customers that bought a full truckload of product

Established Businesses: Integrating a North Star Goal for Sustainability

To understand how established companies are translating North Star goals into executable strategy, let's look at another sustainability innovation that Procter & Gamble undertook. One of P&G's North Star goals was to sell $20 billion of sustainable innovation products.[27] To achieve this goal, P&G would need to translate it into the company's best-selling products, like Tide. Along with its cold-water version of Tide, P&G also created a concentrated formulation of Tide. The effort relied on transparency of information, which demonstrated that another large use of energy (and waste of dollars) was in the transport and production of detergents. The financial returns were clear if P&G could get consumers to switch. Because the bottles were lighter and smaller, millions of dollars in transportation costs could be saved. Because the bottles were smaller, more could fit on the shelf, which meant that the product stayed in stock more easily, which could increase sales.

But here was their challenge. How do you explain that a smaller bottle that costs more is a better deal? To tackle this challenge, Procter & Gamble engaged its marketing team and networked with its longtime partner, Walmart. The retailer itself engaged its associates to figure out how to communicate the benefits of concentrated detergent. Across the country, associates held contests, answered customer questions, and set up display tables to explain the economic and environmental benefits of compact containers of detergent.[28] After lots of tests and prototypes, the employees concluded that the best way to help customers reliably choose the compact version was to fill the entire laundry aisle of the chain's stores with the compact size of every brand, so that consumers could conduct apple-to-apple comparisons between brands. Once Walmart made the switch, consumers began to rave that the bottles weighed less. And although it will never be proved, I like to think that the concentration of laundry detergent relieved a whole lot of back pain across the world.

Act Now: Set Your North Star Goal and Assess Your TEN Cycle

Years of business strategy have trained modern companies to plan out exactly where they're heading before they get started. With the world in a constant state of flux, though, the best you can hope for is to head in the right direction and to prepare your organization for the journey. You can take the following steps:

- Use the STaR map to set a North Star goal and to kick off the idea generation process.

- With that North Star in mind, identify the TEN cycle—the actions that will increase transparency, engagement, and network function—before you determine which product, service, or other idea to pursue.

- Once you launch the initiative, move through the phases of idea generation and idea selection and then move into implementation.

- Write down the state of your TEN cycle (table 3-2). Using the information that you now have, how would you rank the transparency of your organization, the engagement of your employees, and the use of outside networks to improve your organization? Rank your perceived performance from one to ten.

TABLE 3-2

The first steps of setting your TEN cycle in motion

	Transparency	Engagement	Networks
Overall, how would you rank your company's performance on a scale of 1 through 10?			
How would you rank your organization's business units on a scale of 1 through 10? Write down the name of a leader and a laggard:			
How would you rank your competitors on a scale of 1 through 10? Write down the name of a leader and a laggard:			
Quick win: What could you yourself do immediately in each area?			
Game-changer: What could you do in each area, if you got greater management buy-in or support from more colleagues?			
Whose managerial support must you enlist in each area?			
What could you build into your performance goals—for you or your unit—for this fiscal year?			

CHAPTER FOUR

Using Transparency to Execute Your Strategy

Open Up Your Business for Scrutiny

"NO CAMERA, NO PROBLEM," he said, smiling at an attempt at a joke.

I was on a short plane ride with a longtime manager of a meat company. I had just asked him how his industry was reacting to the largest meat recall in American history He was trying to be funny, but I could tell there was a modicum of seriousness in his response. Many of the slaughterhouses he worked with were banning cell phones on the job so that employees could not take and distribute incriminating photographs. No camera, no problem.

The first step in the TEN cycle is transparency, precisely because this kind of control no longer works. So how do you function in a world without secrets? You rush right into it. Not only do you share information with your constituents—from your employees to your customers to your suppliers—but you should also do it *better than* any regulation says you should. Far from posing a threat, this will open your business for ideas and innovations from every crack and crevice of your organization's universe. Transparency is more than just a way to comply with legal responsibilities; it's how you attract societal resources to solve them. By systematically measuring and reporting on your own sustainability, you will engage everyone— again, from your employees to your customers to your suppliers to your critics—in the process of building a truly sustainable enterprise.

In a collection of essays, *Other People's Money—and How the Bankers Use It*, Supreme Court justice Louis Brandeis celebrates the effect of the media on society: "Publicity is justly commended as a remedy for social and industrial diseases."[1] He went on to write: "Sunlight is said to be the best of disinfectants; electric light the most efficient policeman." Being disinfected and policed sounds about as pleasurable as being audited or outsourced. No wonder business leaders typically use the word *transparency* in a legal or corporate relations context and not in terms of business opportunity.

The first step is accepting that information policies that require tight secrecy and control are rapidly obsolescing. Music companies attempted to block university students from downloading music for free and instead lost billions of dollars of market value and music sales. Instead of accepting that the Internet makes the protection of bits of information virtually impossible and developing a business model in which the broader exposure of their artists could be turned into revenue, the music companies threatened to sue their fans. If the companies had put the same energy into creating a new revenue model instead of defending their old way of doing business, they would have a brighter future ahead. And if they had engaged those fans in coming up with a solution to the problem, the industry labels could have found themselves leading the digital revolution instead of becoming one of its victims.

Our society is headed toward sustainability, so if a company is guarding what it is doing, because the activity is unsustainable, the company is eventually likely to find its secret exposed. Better that it figure out how to get some help from the outside world to solve that problem now, whether the problem is real or imagined.[2]

But let's go back to my plane ride. The 2008 Westland/Hallmark recall from that company's Chino, California, slaughterhouse had been broadcast around the world as an example of the failure of the American beef industry to ensure that American beef is safe.[3] This, the largest meat recall in American history, began with an activist who began documenting the daily affairs of a slaughterhouse where he worked undercover for six weeks. He recorded video of cows that appeared too sickly to walk as they were being rolled on a forklift toward slaughter. He recorded a manager hopelessly hitting a cow in the face with a paddle to try to compel it to walk to slaughter. The images were cruel and unnerving.

Once the information got out, it spread like wildfire. The grainy video, distributed by the Humane Society of the United States, quickly dominated the news.

The costs and implications of the scandal were extraordinary. The recall affected over 140 million pounds of beef. Before the recall, Hallmark was the second-largest meat supplier to school lunch programs in the United States. Schools reacted immediately, removing ground beef from their menus out of fear that they had received tainted meat. The San Bernardino district attorney, Michael Ramos, filed charges against employees at the plant and company. "I need the public to understand that my office takes all cases involving animal cruelty very seriously. It doesn't matter whether the mistreated animal is a beloved family pet or a cow at a slaughterhouse," Ramos said.[4]

As my plane trip continued, the meat manager spent a long time venting about the recall. "There's no reason there should have been a recall," he said. "Those cows were probably fine. There was no proof that the cows were diseased." He went on to say that the slaughterhouses he had been to were never like the ones in the video. They were safe and clean, hyperfocused on sanitation and animal welfare.

But for one thing, it is impossible to put the technology genie back in the box. Employers' efforts to seize employees' cell phones or censor their blogs are bound to fail. As are attempts to keep the public eye away from facilities that produce unsafe products or that violate ethical or safety codes. In the end, at least in the court of public opinion, it doesn't really matter whether a meat recall was warranted. If you pit the company's explanations against the videotape, there's no contest.

In the context of those videos, my flight-mate was overlooking that sometimes the question is not if you're right or wrong, but whether you exceed expectations. True transparency isn't living up to a metric; it's a mind-set. The sharing of information above and beyond what is needed is an act of trust that will engage your constituents and enlist them on your behalf. A recall may not have been strictly necessary, but the company implemented one to regain the trust of its customers. And it may never have had to resort to such an extreme measure in the first place if true transparency had been built into the core of its strategy.

Phases and Signs of Greater Transparency

Companies moving toward transparency must shift through four phases, each of which is a step closer to true transparency. These phases are *blind spots, awareness, compliance,* and, finally, *transparency*.

Blind Spots

First, your company should recognize its blind spots, which I define as unanticipated risks or failures—such as the mistreatment of animals in a slaughterhouse. Of course, no company starts out by saying it wants to make products in factories with abusive conditions, but sometimes, a focus on price or a single aspect of quality obscures your vision and prevents you from seeing those abusive conditions.

Outsiders and employees can be useful in identifying these blind spots. Yes, even activists can help you do your job. In 2006, associates and managers began a major new recycling effort at Walmart.

Four phases of transparency

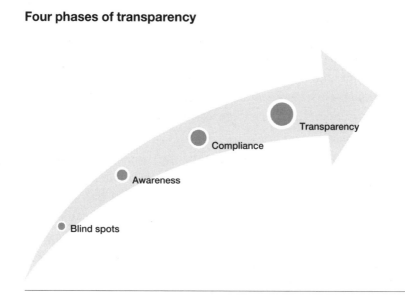

Called Super Sandwich Bale, it was created with the help of Rocky Mountain Recycling.[5] The recycler's idea was simple: use the cardboard baler in the back of the store (which basically crushes cardboard and wraps it with wire) to collect other recyclables in the stores. Associates started collecting and separating plastic hangers, plastic film, aluminum, and other materials, putting them in large plastic bags, and then putting them in the center of a cardboard sandwich and crushing them. The materials were then trucked to recycling centers, separated, and remade into other products.

Incidentally, Walmart now recycles about one-third of what was formerly thrown into the trash compactor—one-third of which is plastic, for which the company has received $350 per ton, plastic that Walmart once paid to have removed from the store. For products that are made out of the polyethylene resin that results from melting down this plastic, it's about half as expensive to use recycled polyethylene resin as it is to use virgin polyethylene resin. And generally speaking, far less carbon dioxide is generated in recycling than in using virgin materials. It was a win-win situation all around.

Sounds pretty good—so where was the blind spot? Right when the national Super Sandwich Bale campaign was being launched, an activist group decided to try to prove that Walmart wasn't actually serious about recycling. The group asked its members to go to a local Walmart, peek into the Dumpster behind the store, and report on the state of recycling in that store.

Walmart could have viewed this activist group as a threat, posting warnings for its managers and rattling the saber of the legal department. But instead, the scrutiny may have reinforced the success of the effort. It's impossible to know for certain, but the possibility that an activist group would make an example of their store as a laggard and an embarrassment to the entire company might have been one good motivator for store managers to kick their recycling efforts into high gear. The challenge for any new program in a large company is encouraging people to come along. How can you use your critics to help reinforce good behavior?

Even when you're only beginning to recognize your blind spots, you're beginning to build a culture that recognizes that you might not be as smart as you think you are. This humble view of the world outside your walls encourages you to constantly innovate. Pulling energy-intensive processes out of a supply chain or reducing the amount of resources required in a product will take innovation. If I had a dollar for every time a company has asked me to get an aspect of its supply chain fixed by putting out a request for a proposal (RFP), I'd be a very rich man. But rarely will material challenges be solved by an RFP; if the substitutes were all available immediately at the same price, then everyone would be using them. Instead of seeing the problem as unique, you can benefit from relying on the wisdom of crowds (the idea that the aggregation of a larger number of individual opinions has a better chance of being right than any singular opinion) or crowd sourcing (the idea that you can use the ideas in the crowd to drive your business forward). Companies like Procter & Gamble have long since abandoned the idea that innovation must come from within. These companies regularly go out and purchase new consumer innovations and use their distribution system to help themselves reach their potential.

Starbucks recently introduced a new line of "ready-to-make" coffee, which is a fancy way of describing instant coffee. Starbucks has exacting standards for its brew and had been wary of releasing anything that wasn't up to its quality standards. The invention of this new product came from a customer who loved to go camping. His wife refused to go, though, unless she could get a good cup of coffee. At some point, he became tired of filling his backpack with tools for brewing. He began inventing. In his kitchen, he started prebrewing cups of coffee and then removing the water and freezing the brew. He then would scrape it and pack it in. His wife was quite happy. One day, he shared his invention with a local Starbucks manager, who took it all the way to Starbucks CEO Howard Schultz. Schultz hired the inventor as the head of R&D.[6]

Crowd sourcing works. Consider the television show *Who Wants to Be a Millionaire?* The ask-the-audience lifeline—when the contestant chooses to follow the advice of the studio audience— is the only foolproof way to get the right answer. In *The Professor and the Madman*, Simon Winchester cunningly tells the story of one of the thousands of citizen volunteers (one in an asylum for the criminally insane) who collectively wrote the *Oxford English Dictionary* by sending in millions of slips of paper with definitions and the original sources of all the known words in the English language.[7]

There are three main benefits of using the wisdom of the public to help your company build your strategy for sustainability.

1. You get a bigger team. You can reach beyond the talents of your own organization.

2. It's cheap. You pay only for results, unlike your own R&D efforts.

3. You can examine multiple avenues simultaneously.

The first step is saying "what's so." It sounds obvious, but sharing your problems is the first step toward transparency. What happens when you start sharing the real state of affairs? Usually it's a cathartic experience; it allows reinvention, reduces complacency, and socializes the problems, which allows people inside and outside of the company to act. It takes the monkey off your employees' backs and allows it to run around the forest on its own for a while. Instead of protecting information, your company makes the information useful; in the process, you give critics a chance to offer solutions instead of critiques.

Why is finding your own faults important? The psychologist Abraham Maslow said, "If you plan on being anything less than you are capable of being, you will probably be unhappy all the days of your life." Although it's hard to face sometimes, critiques present an opportunity to improve. A healthy company feasts on the contents of its errors as opportunities to improve.

Awareness

The second step toward transparency is awareness. In this step, you begin to catalog and assess blind spots to understand whether they are episodic or systemic. Is there an underlying cause? If so, how can it be removed or altered so that the risk of failure is mitigated? Companies should also use this period to audit their own performance: by looking at the whole of what they've found, can they see any holes in their search? Are there patterns that could lead them to identify more potential problem spots? At this point, you need to discover and sort through all the bad news you possibly can.

Compliance

The third step is compliance. Most companies stop here (or, at the very least, only aim this high). In this step, they compare their former blind spots with relevant laws, regulations, and industry behaviors and work to meet those standards. The regulatory standards represent the legal minimum that they must reach.

But it is not enough. Companies need to exceed expectations; in sustainability, they must go above and beyond. Sustainability is not just a box to be checked off. Take Apple, for example. Apple's customers tend to be highly concerned with sustainability issues—while the company has appeared less focused on the issues, despite the claims in its advertisements. In 2006, when Greenpeace started ranking cell phone and computer companies according to their use of toxic substances and their commitment to recycling electronic waste, Apple was near the bottom of the pack.[8] One of the chemicals that Apple had been using was brominated flame retardants. In the 1970s, a whole class of fire retardants called polybrominated biphenyls (PBBs) was taken off the market after a bag of Firemaster FF-1, a commercial PBB, was accidentally mistaken for animal feed and poisoned thousands of Michigan farm animals. Today's flame retardants are much less toxic, but recent research has suggested that there may be accumulations of brominated flame retardants in humans and other animals. As a result, people have become concerned about the potential harmful effects of this class of chemicals, since little research exists to show that PBBs are safe.[9]

Greenpeace also ranked technology companies according to their efforts to increase energy efficiency and to take back and recycle outdated equipment. In early rankings, Apple slid down the list as companies like Dell and Lenovo began to increase their efforts. Thinking that Apple would make a good target, Greenpeace used classic network tools to encourage Apple's own customers to put pressure on Apple:

> *We want you to run this campaign. We want you to create the campaign T-shirt, pen the speech in which Steve Jobs announces the Greening of Apple, shoot the Apple ad that sets Cupertino talking about clean production and take-back schemes.*
>   *The Green my Apple site has all the information and raw materials you need to get you started. If you're creative, create.*

If you're networked, network. There's plenty to do, and many hands make light work.[10]

Greenpeace gave away Creative Commons licenses to its award-winning photographs in order to give the network the tools to carry out the campaign.[11]Apple fans responded, creating Web sites, T-shirts, blogs, and other commentaries that put pressure on the company.

Apple's response was almost universally defensive, attacking Greenpeace as if the organization had it wrong and claiming to be at least no worse than Apple's competitors. When Greenpeace rented a booth at the UK MacExpo, the organizers of the convention shut it down. Greenpeace created a YouTube "alternative" keynote to Jobs's famous speeches at the expo. In the alternative, the fictitious Jobs announced the phaseout of dangerous chemicals, a worldwide computer take-back policy, and an iPod that was recycled and recyclable as well as powered by solar and kinetic energy.[12]

After months of trying to ignore the attacks or silence them, Jobs finally posted a letter entitled "A Greener Apple." The letter seemed like a nonapology apology from a teenager to a parent. In the letter, Jobs apologizes for not sharing all the good things Apple is doing:

Apple has been criticized by some environmental organizations for not being a leader in removing toxic chemicals from its new products, and for not aggressively or properly recycling its old products. Upon investigating Apple's current practices and progress towards these goals, I was surprised to learn that in many cases Apple is ahead of, or will soon be ahead of, most of its competitors in these areas. Whatever other improvements we need to make, it is certainly clear that we have failed to communicate the things that we are doing well.[13]

He goes on to detail some good initiatives that bring Apple firmly up to the middle of the pack of electronics makers. Not as good as Sony, but not as bad as Nintendo.

Jobs is unquestionably one of the most innovative CEOs of our generation. But instead of asking for help or declaring a leadership position or creating a leap forward as revolutionary as the Macintosh or the iPhone, in this case he merely goes as far as complying with the most basic expectations of companies. It appears that for Jobs, sustainability is not a business opportunity, but rather a risk to be mitigated. Recently, Apple has improved its performance, with new MacBook models reducing many toxic components. The new models feature arsenic-free glass, no mercury, no brominated flame retardants, and no polyvinyl chloride; they also feature shells made of recyclable aluminum and glass. In addition, the models have backlit screens that are 30 percent more efficient than the traditional liquid crystal display (LCD). Apple hasn't given credit at all to Greenpeace for these steps, but it seems likely that the Greenpeace campaign had an effect. Even with these steps, Apple is not living up to its potential. Apple Computer, Inc., should be redefining planned obsolescence, but instead, it's making only incremental progress. Great companies deserve great expectations.[14]

Jobs should have known that the Greenpeace campaign would catch fire. Distributed technologies, from cell phone cameras to Wi-Fi to YouTube, make it impossible to control information centrally as a corporation. Instead of investing time in trying to suppress discussion or debate, Jobs could have addressed customers' concerns head-on and worked with people both inside and outside the company to identify the problems at the root of those concerns, and to solve them.

Transparency

The final step is true transparency itself, and it is the one that most companies miss and the one that makes all the difference. Beyond bringing operations into compliance, share the information broadly inside and outside an organization. This will allow a company to open up opportunities for further improvements and innovations that it probably never even considered—some from the same individuals who pointed out its blind spots, and some from newer contributors. By widely sharing information about the failure, the company will ensure that employees learn from the situation, it will gain the trust of its employees, and it will be able to tap the innovation resources of everyone whom you've engaged.

Time Is Money, and Transparency Is Time

So what does transparency get you that compliance doesn't? Chairman of the Sierra Club Carl Pope believes that transparency "is the only way we're going to change the marketplace fast enough to get out of the climate crisis."[15] Pope raised eyebrows when he engineered the endorsement of the Clorox Green Works products by the Sierra Club. He had spent his career advocating and creating warning labels that kept people away from environmentally hazardous products, and here he was, putting a Sierra Club logo on household cleaners, trying to get those same people to buy Clorox products. Pope is quick to point out that Green Works lists its ingredients, even though it's not required to by any regulation.

According to Pope, transparency comes naturally to some: "Companies that seek to remain innovative, high-performance market leaders find it fairly easy to get it that transparency works and to act on it. Those that are trying to eke out profits by being low-cost innovation laggards won't ever get it." Because the first thing that nontransparent companies are wasting is their own time.

New United Motor Manufacturing, Inc., or NUMMI, was formed through a historic alliance between Toyota and General Motors in 1984. The idea was for GM to learn more about the lean production model of Toyota, and for Toyota to test its production methods in an American context. According to Pope, when Toyota took over the existing General Motors plant, the Japanese company found a major crack in the paint bay; chemicals had been leaking through the crack for years. General Motors hadn't known the crack was there. When the new plant managers were called in to look, they told the staff, most of whom had worked for GM for years, to call the Environmental Protection Agency (EPA) and find out what the agency wanted them to do. The former GM staff were stunned. In the GM culture, the response would have been to call the lawyers, not the EPA. There's a saying in Japan: "Fix the problem, not the blame." And in this case, NUMMI's focus was on disclosing the problem and solving it.

Three years later, Toyota wanted to get air permits for a new truck assembly line. The permits would allow for one of the biggest new sources of air pollution in the San Francisco Bay area in years, in an area where it's tough to get permits of any kind. Toyota got its permit in an unprecedented six months. According to Pope, the automaker's earlier openness had earned it the community support it needed for the permit.

"Time is money. Transparency is time," said Pope.

True transparency goes beyond complying with laws and regulations—that's only scratching the surface. Transparency and openness are business opportunities. Historically, openness and transparency have been viewed mainly in a regulatory context. Companies are compelled to comply with their legal responsibilities. But why not be proactive about it? Welcoming, even. In other words, why not engage critics and ask them to help make the company better?

Nike's Blind Spot and the Creation of Awareness

Let's follow one company along the path from sustainability blind spots to transparency. In a little over ten years, Nike has morphed from a company stained by human rights abuses into a company that is becoming known for thoughtful product design and transparency. Through its Considered line, Nike is bringing core concepts of sustainability into its business practices. How did this evolution happen?

Nike becomes aware of its blind spots. As a response to rising U.S. wages during the mid-1980s, Nike closed its U.S. factories and began outsourcing manufacturing to Asia, where wages are cheap and labor laws are, shall we say, variably enforced.

Michael Shellenberger, an author and a strategist who worked with the antisweatshop activist Jeff Ballinger and Global Exchange to launch the anti-Nike campaign, described their attraction to Nike as a target: "We saw it as a way to talk about globalization." Shellenberger paused and chuckled, "Which, at the time, I was against."[16]

The attacks were piercing. The activists accused Nike of subjecting subcontracted employees to human rights abuses ranging from inadequate wages to child labor. They had an opportunity to attack Nike because of its public perception. "There was a sense that they were held to a higher standard by their consumers and that would be an advantage to us," Shellenberger said.

The group of activists, pulled together by United Students Against Sweatshops and Global Exchange, launched protests and sit-ins that swept campuses across the country. Protesters demanded that Nike reform its practices and institute a monitoring system to ensure that these reforms stuck.

One of the group's most successful efforts was to attack something Nike prided itself on—its support of women's involvement in sports. "We did a sign-on letter with women's groups around Nike's empowerment of women at home while exploiting women abroad," Shellenberger said. "It caught on like wildfire. People really responded to a company that seemed to have a double standard for here and abroad."

Activists, then, were the outsider blind-spot finders for Nike. They publicly charged Nike with these failures.

Nike moves to compliance. In 1997, Nike decided to become part of the White House Apparel Industry Group, a presidential task force composed of labor and human rights groups, governments, and competitors like Reebok. Together, they agreed to set new standards to improve conditions in contract factories. The new code specified conduct on wages and working conditions. It included a maximum sixty-hour workweek for apparel factories—a standard that many American companies now use around the world. They also committed to support a group of oversee monitors who would inspect apparel factories worldwide and provide audits on their findings.[17] To make sure rigorous monitoring continued overseas, the task force also created an association to preside over apparel factory inspectors and piloted a certificate of compliance program for those companies that complied with the code of conduct.

Nike moves to transparency. In the late 1990s, Nike launched a thorough investigation of environmental and labor conditions in the factories that create Nike products.[18] The company joined the Fair Labor Association—a monitoring outfit it founded with human rights groups and other companies—and now allows inspections of its facilities. Since then, Nike has formed an in-house team, which inspects an average of three hundred factories per year, grading them on labor standards.[19] These audit tools are now public. In 2004, Nike voluntarily published the names and addresses of all its contract factories. Nike's supply-chain transparency allows full disclosure of all seven hundred factories in which Nike products are produced.

In moving from transparency as a "have to" to a "want to," Nike had passed the transparency test.

Nike "Considered"

But Nike is a company based on performance. How does its commitment to transparency affect its business strategy? Each season, Nike CEO Mark Parker asks one question of his designers: "Tell me how this shoe performs better than the year before." For Nike, the move from sustainability as a way of complying with social expectations to sustainability as a business strategy was epitomized by the addition of another question: "How is this shoe more sustainable than the year before?"

Lorrie Vogel joined Nike in 1997 and works with the Considered team at Nike, the group responsible for sustainability initiatives at the company. "We wanted one group that was the central point," she said, explaining how the Considered team was tasked with minimizing Nike's footprint.[20] Unlike many other companies, where the corporate social responsibility group is mostly concerned with reports and speaking at conferences, Considered is a central business-service group, supporting Nike's categories. Vogel's key role was to take the multitude of environmental programs and tie them into the business.

"At first we asked the designers to design a sustainable shoe," she said. The challenge proved too broad and amorphous. "They froze because it was an impossible challenge; they didn't know where to start. Then we said, just choose one thing to make it more sustainable than it was the year before." This small-step approach began to get traction.

Transparency can make a company better on the inside. The Considered team started laying out a measurement system to make the sustainability of shoes transparent to the designers who create them. Nike used transparency to improve its internal performance, not just to make outsiders feel better. "We gave the design teams a specific series of choices that could help their designs become internally certified as a Considered product," said Vogel.

The Considered group set up four major goals:

1. Produce products with less waste.

2. Use fewer toxic substances.

3. Choose more environmentally friendly materials.

4. Design product with sustainable innovation.

Each of the goals has a set of philosophies and business strategies behind it. The goal of producing products with less waste, for example, was tied to clear financial goals. "We look at anything that doesn't end up in a consumer's closet as waste," said Vogel. Nike calculates an estimated annual value of around $800 million dollars of waste that could eventually be reduced through the Considered initiative.

What makes Nike so transparent is the metric scoring system that designers use to understand the sustainability score of each shoe that they are working on. When a shoe is created at Nike, the designer hands the design to a "developer," who builds the shoe into a set of specifications through a bill of materials that is connected to an automated scoring system. It's at this point that the materials are questioned. What kind of upper could be used with this pattern? What type of midsole? What type of outsole? What type of materials are being used throughout the product?

By entering the specifications into the system, the developer can see how they're scoring. If the specs are getting a poor score on pattern efficiency, the developer can go back to parting lines (the place where the patterns are cut) and move them. The software prompts the developer to calculate the pattern efficiency, gives guidance on more environmentally friendly materials, and recommends less toxic substances. Based on the developer's choices, each shoe is assigned a Considered ranking of gold, silver, bronze, or "not considered." Designers and developers can get additional points if they come up with a new innovation. And they receive "early adopter" bonus points if they're early to implement a new innovation. Nike gives this bonus so that there's no "not invented here" mentality. In the competitive culture of the company, the Considered group wants to encourage the borrowing of other people's ideas to implement good ideas faster.

Nike has committed to having 100 percent of its footwear meet baseline Considered standards by 2011. This equates to real numbers. That's a 20 percent increase in environmentally preferred materials. A 17 percent reduction in waste. And maintaining their reduction of volatile organic compounds—VOCs—at 95 percent. In shoes, the main source of toxic VOCs is adhesives, and Nike has been a leader in creating new water-based adhesives. "As soon as you set goals, it's amazing how quickly people hit them," Vogel said.

Doing More and Talking Less

It's this internal transparency that is the key step, not the "transparency" of public relations. For Nike, one of the savviest marketers on the planet, the sustainable aspects of its shoes have been missing from its external marketing efforts. Said Vogel, "People don't come to Nike because they want green. They come because they want the best performance." She believes passionately that sustainability only works when it moves the core brand proposition forward. In the case of Nike, sustainability is all about how to make a better shoe, like adding a carbon fiber plate with a water-based adhesive. "There will never will be a sacrifice in performance to make a Considered product. That's the best way to kill the movement," said Vogel.

The transformation of a company from one focused on protecting itself from public scrutiny to one that leads while keeping its head down, and not trumpeting a "green" or "sustainable" message, is a remarkable one. Vogel explained, "We focus on transparency and doing the work rather than talking about the work." She paused when I asked her about how things have changed at Nike. "We're doing more and talking less," she said.

Nutrition Information: Measuring and Reporting

Of course, talking isn't necessarily a bad thing, and external transparency is valuable, too. You should enable your customers and other constituencies to know as much as possible about your products. As a way to bring customers into their networks, many companies are voluntarily reporting on the materials that go into their manufacturing.

For example, when you open a box of the new Timberland Earthkeeper shoes, you find an ingredients label that includes the environmental impacts associated with the production of the shoe. It's a lot like a nutritional label on food packaging—except it's not required. This is a story about a shoe company that has used this kind of transparency as a way to engage customers in the life of their shoes.

Take the 2009 Earthkeeper 2.0 Boot, for example, which gets a score of 7.5 on Timberland's Green Index. The product specific score on the overall nutrition label reveals both a recycled content of about 25 percent and a carbon footprint of about 75 kilograms for this particular model. The climate score is 7.5 since Timberland's carbon footprint models show an impact of 75 kilograms of CO_2 for materials and manufacturing. The Chemicals score is 7.5, since solvent-based adhesives are used in all three main construction points in the boot. The Resources score also happens to be a 7.5 since 25 percent of the shoe is recycled or renewable (75 percent non-recycled or nonrenewable).

It took a few years to get the labeling system to this level of detail. Timberland, like many companies, is linked in a complex supply chain to hundreds of factory partners; they use material from thousands of suppliers.[21] When the program started in 2006, it was a challenge to collect all the data needed to rate the impact of the shoes, so Timberland started by reporting on its carbon footprint. But the company wanted the information to be specific to each individual shoe style, so it worked with stakeholders to decide the metrics and criteria for what would be called the Green Index.

The Green Index rates a shoe on a scale one to ten—measuring its contribution to climate change (through analyses of the shoe's life cycle, from raw materials through production to finished product), chemical use, and resource consumption (the proportion of recycled, organic, or renewable materials that were consumed in the making of the shoe).

What does the consumer think of all this information? Betsy Blaisdell, Timberland's manager of environmental stewardship, told me, "Consumers say, 'Oh cool, you're being transparent about the good things and the bad things' . . . PVC plastic being present, solvent-based adhesives being present. I think companies who share the good with the bad will win with the consumer. It increases your credibility, and you become a trusted source for information."[22]

All of this labeling and measuring gives people information they can use to make better decisions about what products to buy on the basis of what they value. The measurements also help Timberland gauge how it is meeting its own internal goals for reducing resource consumption and saving energy, while finding ways to win with the consumer in the process.

"The real a-ha was that it wasn't about *adding* green bells and whistles—organic, hemp, etc.—it was about simplifying our design. Do we have to have anti-microbial agents in our shoes? Do we need linings? There's a direct connection between weight of the product and greenhouse gas emissions, and less weight means less cost associated with shipping. And it turns out consumers want high-performance shoes that are lightweight," Blaisdell said.

Timberland is meeting its financial goals as well. Even in a challenging operating environment it grew its income from $40 million in 2007 to $42.9 in 2008.[23] It is too soon to tell how the tag figures into purchase intent. In the beginning, Timberland put the label on the box, so consumers didn't see it until after they had already bought the shoes. Now the label is on the bottom of the shoe. "For us the true measure of success will be whether the rest of the industry adopts or emulates what we've done. The label is useful in only a limited way, unless shoppers can use it to compare with different items," said Blaisdell.

Timberland's CEO Jeffrey Swartz is not shy about his passion for sustainable business. He has declared his belief: "Our industry can become carbon neutral as fast as we demand it. We have the ability to say I *won't* buy fashion where the chemicals that are used pollute the environment, and I *will* do business with companies that are thoughtful about their carbon footprint. You watch. It will be the most powerful, popular uprising that corporate America ever saw, because we are motivated to deliver results."[24]

Sustainability does benefit society, but that's not the reason most businesses exist. They exist to build value for their shareholders. While some people might find this distasteful, that's the reality. Sustainability isn't about choosing against the shareholder's interest; it's a way of doing business, an approach that builds more value for the shareholder by incorporating new trends, opportunities, and risks into the field of view. So how do you measure and report on that value in a way that maximizes transparency?

One of the first ways that businesses began to talk about the market opportunities from being a good corporate citizen was through the idea of a triple bottom line. "Having coined the term in 1994, it took three to four years to get businesspeople to accept the concept, which they tended to see as much more challenging than *eco-efficiency*," said John Elkington, a corporate environmental consultant for more than twenty years.[25]

The *triple bottom line* refers to the costs and values associated with doing business in terms beyond the traditional measures of accounting. Through this perspective, environmental and social costs are measured alongside purely financial gauges. The triple bottom line can be thought of as three overlapping sectors of concern: people (human capital), planet (environmental systems health), and profit (the economic outcome, shared by all), with sustainability as the end goal. For the purposes of this book and my definition of sustainability, I've added the fourth factor of culture. The trend toward maintaining cultural integrity in a globalized world will only be increased by rising fuel costs, which will

The sustainable bottom line

Integrating internal management and external conditions for long-term profitability

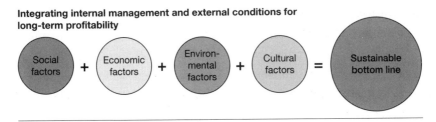

encourage local production. The idea of making a quadruple bottom line seems a bit silly, so we can simply call it a *sustainable bottom line*.

Although the triple bottom line was created to inspire innovation, Elkington fears that it is now more of a stand-in for another form of mere compliance. "For me," he said, "the original purpose of the triple bottom line was as a provocation and as a way of making the complexity of the sustainability concept at least a little more intelligible for business brains."

What are the challenges of maintaining the integrity of the triple bottom line?

"Well," said Elkington, "it's easy for companies to take advantage of using the inevitable trade-offs across the three main domains of value added or destroyed to cover their flanks. There is also the presence of an inadequate understanding of the difference between a financial and wider economic bottom line, and a sometimes almost willful avoidance of the social dimension." The challenge in any kind of measuring and reporting is to find useful standards of measurement—and then to exceed them.

So, What Should You Measure?

Find a measurement that matters to the business, and measure that. For a transport-heavy business, fuel usage is a good measurement. In education, measure how much sustainability knowledge is produced in students. For a retail business that has a large labor force, measure how sustainability helps in the hiring and retention of staff. For a fashion business, measure how sustainability can help inspire the most creative designs. Table 4-1 gives examples of specific metrics to track within the four categories of sustainability.

There are a number of "check the box" questions you'll need to answer: the amount of natural light in buildings, whether there is a recycling program, where energy is derived from. But, in the end,

TABLE 4-1

Examples of specific measurements for tracking sustainability

Category	Description	Specific measurement to be tracked
Social	Actions that can affect all members of society; category includes poverty, violence, injustice, education, health care, and labor and human rights	• Accidents per hour of work • Product safety ratings • Anticorruption practices • Performance on transparency in labeling, as determined by outside rating agencies
Economic	Actions that affect how humans meet their basic needs; category includes employment opportunities, access to health care, and safe housing	• Revenue growth • Margin percentage • Revenue per employee • Reserves for future expenses • Customer satisfaction
Environmental	Actions that affect Earth's ecology; category includes climate change, preservation of natural resources, carbon footprint, and conservation	• Materials used by weight or volume per dollar of revenue • Percentage of recycled input materials used • Energy use per unit of revenue • Percentage of locally customized products or service offerings • Energy saved from conservation and efficiency • Total water use • Percentage and total volume of water recycled and reused • Total direct and indirect greenhouse gas emissions by weight • Negative effects on biodiversity • Annual transportation costs
Cultural	Actions through which communities manifest identity and preserve and cultivate traditions and customs from generation to generation	• Visits to suppliers • Hours of training and development per employee per year • Percentage of products bought from within 500 miles of locations • Employee retention • Percentage of employees covered by excellent health-care benefits • Cultural diversity of workforce • Distinctly cultural traditions

these are relatively easy to solve for—the big question is how to make the business better.

The Global Reporting Initiative, the de facto global standard for sustainability reporting, uses the following factors as a guide to determine materiality for reporting:

- Key organizational values, policies, strategies, operational management systems, goals, and targets (e.g., employees, shareholders, and suppliers)

- The interests and expectations of stakeholders specifically invested in the success of the organization

- Significant risks to the organization

- Critical factors for organizational success

- The core competencies of the organization and how they can or could contribute to sustainable development[26]

The ongoing problem with compliance, as we've seen, is that it often manifests as complacency—the enemy of innovation. Compliance implies that you are meeting the base standards. There is a profound difference between moving away from the bad and going toward the good. In avoiding the bad, the focus is centered on failure. Subsequent action is dominated by fear. In striving for the good, you invite hope and demand the creation of a new path.

Reporting

Once you are tracking the right metrics, how do you get the information into the right hands? The following discussion points out that there are even pitfalls in tracking the right measurements.

It's not about a report. As with the measurements themselves, sustainability reports have become enablers of mere compliance—blanket descriptions for the ways that corporations report their nonfinancial information. Corporate social responsibility (CSR) reports; or environment, health, and safety (EHS) reports; or even triple-bottom-line reports are subject to the pitfalls of compliance-oriented, lowest-standard thinking. Sustainability reporting should be woven into the core financial reports that a business makes. There are only a handful of Wall Street investors who invest according to the triple-bottom-line performance of a company. There is only one bottom line—the profitability of a corporation. If what a company is doing for sustainability doesn't lead to sustained cash returns, then the company's strategy probably needs to be rethought.

In recent years, Goldman Sachs has tracked the performance of companies using a framework it calls GS Sustain, which emphasizes performance across environmental, social, and governance (ESG) issues. It has consistently found that companies with top-quartile performance against the Goldman Sachs ESG screens have above-average ratios of cash return on capital invested (CROCI).[27] CROCI is an effective way of putting a magnifying glass on the singular bottom line I describe earlier, because while growth is often fleeting for companies after a new product line or market matures, consistent cash returns that take into account the costs of capital are the surest economic sign of a company that has a sustainable bottom line. Add to that a view of the four aspects of sustainability (social, economic, environmental, and cultural), or ESG issues, and you've got a complete picture of the sustainable bottom line.

Not surprisingly, Goldman Sachs cares deeply about transparency. It writes that, "Disclosure affects performance. Some companies do not view ESG impacts as sufficiently material to company performance to warrant quantification and public disclosure and therefore do not publish performance indicators. However, we believe that the indicators we use to assess performance with respect to environmental, social and corporate governance issues are essential to analyze a company's ability to sustain competitive advantage over the long term. We therefore penalize companies that do not disclose ESG data with the lowest score."[28]

Sustainability reports were born of the social reporting done by German companies in the 1970s.[29] In the 1980s, nonfinancial reports became more common in the United States as community right-to-know regulations connected to the Superfund legislation (which governed the cleanup of toxic waste sites) required more disclosure by corporations. But it wasn't until recently that the reports became a social requirement for *Fortune* 1000 companies. If a company wasn't producing a report, there was bound to be a shareholder resolution demanding that a report be created.[30]

Sustainability reports play a role in helping raise the visibility of sustainability in the corporation, but they often serve to reinforce the impression that sustainability is a social responsibility, not a business strategy. The skills that it takes to write a report are not necessarily the skills it takes to run a good business initiative. In the companies that see the writing of their report as a major part of their sustainability initiative, the people they hire are good at audits, processes, and community relations. That's all fine, except that companies need people who are good at innovation, marketing, and change management if they want a successful business initiative. The litmus test should be this: What you choose to measure and report should be connected to something you already track in the business and should be connected to someone's business role.

Building Transparency into the Culture of Your Business

As companies move down the path of the four steps to transparency, they need to watch out for false transparency. Ironically, the statements that many companies use to demonstrate their transparency are barriers to actually being transparent. You want to watch out for these: companies need truth, not truisms. If an organization confines discussions of transparency to the legal and corporate affairs departments, and if it's generally spoken about in glowing terms, the company's efforts towards transparency are probably misaligned. While sharing information outside the company is important, sharing within the organization should be the first priority. And if you're deliberately spending a lot of effort to hide bad news from your staff, don't waste the effort. Only by owning up to the bad news can companies make the good stuff happen. For years, GE denied its responsibility for pollution of the Hudson River, spending millions of dollars on lawsuits on the efforts while simultaneously claiming that it was a passionate steward of the environment. Only by settling the case could GE establish its sustainability credentials and begin the hard work of transforming a large industrial conglomerate.[31]

Instead, the key to building transparency into the core is constant communications surrounding transparency itself. The goal of transparency—of exceeding expectations of openness—needs to be demonstrated in every report, every speech, every product label, every meeting, and every building. The organization's task is to make transparency not just a procedural point, but also a part of its culture. There is the threat that an employee who does not have the company's best interest at heart will use all this available information in a way that could be harmful, like compiling and publicizing company failures without any context. That's one reason why transparency requires robust employee engagement.

Consider the way that many companies build buy-in for safety. They hold safety moments at the beginning of meetings, ensuring that everyone knows where the doors are. If an employee sees a spilled glass of water, he or she has been trained to ask a friend to stand watch (to ensure no one slips) while the employee goes to get a towel.[32] There is a similar opportunity for this kind of employee participation with transparency. How are they sharing facts about their work within every communication? DuPont has worked to transform its safety-based culture into a sustainability-oriented culture by holding town meetings with insiders and outsiders, declaring sustainability "marketplace" goals, like "By 2015, DuPont will nearly double revenues from non-depletable resources to at least $8 billion."[33] Such meetings make sustainability actionable for a large swath of the company. DuPont has also created Sustainable Growth Excellence Awards, to reward "teams that have created shareholder and societal value while reducing the environmental footprint along our value chains."[34] The awards follow the model of DuPont's annual safety awards.

Not surprisingly, to drive the goal of transparency home, a link to compensation is very handy. At Duke Energy, top executives' pay is tied to the achievement of clearly published operational sustainability metrics.[35] These incentives must touch not just the salaries of company strategists, but also the performance goals of each employee. Companies like Walmart democratize their sales data by pushing it all the way down the chain so that associates in the aisles know how their store is doing and whether they're heading for a bonus. Transparency is a part of a sustainability effort because if this kind of visibility is built into the compensation system, then every employee will understand his or her contribution to the company's sustainability goals and will know if they're being achieved.

Successfully transparent organizations begin teaching the value of transparency at the very beginning of employment. They'll discuss it in new-hire induction; they'll give new employees a chance to ask the CEO any questions. They'll openly discuss their organizational challenges in the hiring process, so that new hires know what they're getting. The tone for transparency needs to be set from the moment someone applies for a job. Disney and the Four Seasons Hotels have multiday orientation programs to ensure that new hires understand the values and the expectations of the company. Bloomberg gives all the new hires a book, *The Bloomberg Way*, and tests them before they begin. Goldman Sachs has a program for the first one hundred days of a new employee's work life. All of these companies involve and inform their employees in the company's culture and strategy.

At the same time, a transparent organization is modeled first and foremost by the CEO and the company leadership. The test? Do staff members believe that management is open and honest with them? To be a transparent leader, you should observe these practices:

1. Quickly deliver company news, whether it's good or bad.

2. Publicly embrace all environmental expectations (don't drive a Hummer if you're asking the company to act like a Prius).

3. Celebrate examples when team members find ways to share actionable data.

For example, Richard Branson is the "innovator in chief" for his Virgin Group brands. He expects his employees to be innovative and deliberately sets an example through well-publicized activities from biofuel test flights to adventure travel. Mitsubishi's CEO Ryoichi Ueda appointed himself the company's chief sustainability officer in 2008, sending a signal that the company, which has been attacked for its global forest practices, would show leadership from the top.

Finally, transparency also needs to be built into the products and how they're sold. If it's a service, is the pricing clear and fair; do clients understand the value equation? If it's a food product, are the ingredients clearly listed and with as much useful detail as possible? Can consumers go to a Web site to learn more and ask questions? Is there a clear policy on what ingredients will never be used, and why? In all actions, are employees guided by a strict non-corruption standard, promising that the company will never do anything illegal or untoward to win a piece of business? Well-known certifications like USDA Organic or Fair Trade are a good place to start for sustainable certifications.

Transparency is a way of operating that comes naturally to people who were born into a world with Facebook and Twitter broadcasting details that would normally have remained private. But it can also be learned, and it can provide a foundation that helps engage employees in your efforts to building a sustainable enterprise.

Act Now: Choose and Use Dipsticks

Here is a so-called dipstick test—a good, quick gauge of your company's level of sustainability:

1. Pick three employees at different levels in the company and ask them (a) What are the top three priorities of the company? (b) What are the three greatest challenges

we face? (c) What is the biggest risk facing our core product or service? (d) Do these risks and challenges make sense to you? Are you working towards resolving these issues?

2. Now, poll three nonprofit leaders who serve as watchdogs for your industry. Ask them (a) What do you think we could be doing better? (b) In our industry, is there another company that is doing better, and if so, why? (c) What information would you like to know about us?

3. Finally, talk to three customers. Ask them (a) Do you have any concerns about our products and services? (b) What's your favorite brand, and why? (c) Do you feel as if you get enough information about our company?

CHAPTER FIVE

Engaging Individuals

People Want to Help

HAVE YOU EVER played in a tide pool? My kids love them. The kids splash around in those intertidal zones between the Pacific Ocean and the California coast, peering into pools that teem with otherworldly species like sea anemones and starfish. The mussels fascinate me. From high tide to low tide, wave after wave, these little creatures can cling to rocks on the shore or to the hulls of ships on high seas. What makes them stick? Tiny threads called byssus hairs, tentacles that can grow to over an inch long, affix themselves to almost any surface. They're better than any glue. Biochemists at the University of Oregon studied byssus at a molecular level and figured out how to replicate this "glue" using other proteins.[1] One day, this mussel-inspired glue could replace the toxic formaldehyde-based glue that manufacturers use to make plywood, which releases its hold when wet. Byssus-style glue can maintain its stickiness through hours of boiling in hot water.

Compared with a human being, a mussel is a fantastically simple organism. Our own capacity to "make things stick" when trends ebb and flow far exceeds the mussel's and derives its strength from our social and cultural tentacles, our interactions with the people in our lives. Engaging and empowering these daily personal connections are critical to executing any corporate strategy for sustainability. While STaR mapping, scenario planning, and North Star goal setting are global and organizational, the execution of strategy is local and personal. Fail your people, and you fail your plan.

That's why in this chapter, we'll discuss engaging your employees. As an example of "making it stick," we'll look at the personal sustainability project that we started with Walmart's employees. You will see the integration of personal and corporate strategic goals—and what a difference the integration can make in your business and in the world.

Does Your Roof Leak? Where, Why, and with What Effect?

"Look for the 2111," parents advised each other to protect their children from a tainted batch of peanut butter. Millions of jars coded 2111 from a single facility in Sylvester, Georgia, had been contaminated with salmonella, a group of bacteria that can cause a common food-borne illness whose symptoms include fever, diarrhea, and abdominal cramps. If you have a weakened immune system, then a peanut-butter-and-jelly-and-salmonella sandwich can kill you.

ConAgra, the company that makes Peter Pan peanut butter, scrambled to respond. It recalled its peanut butter from store shelves and released statements to calm the nerves of the six hundred people whom Peter Pan had sickened in the United States. "We are truly sorry for any harm that our peanut butter products may have caused," said Gary Rodkin, CEO of ConAgra.[2] But the damage had been done.

Equally mortifying, a salmonella outbreak in peanut butter was extremely rare. To make peanut butter, the manufacturing plant cooks ingredients to a temperature of 300 degrees, which should kill salmonella. Had there evolved a new superstrain of salmonella that could withstand those temperatures?

The actual culprit turned out to be nothing more exotic than poor sanitation, a leaky roof, and a faulty sprinkler system. Most likely, water had simply seeped into the vats of peanut butter, allowing bacteria to grow. But the problem went deeper than that. Dozens, maybe hundreds, of workers and managers walked past this leaky roof every day and never cared enough nor felt empowered enough to say or do anything about it. And in 2009, the entire episode was repeated, with tens of thousands of people sickened by more salmonella-contaminated peanut butter at a Blakely, Georgia, manufacturing plant, just seventy-five miles from the last major peanut butter-related salmonella outbreak. According to the *New York Times*, "Raw peanuts were stored next to the finished peanut butter. The roaster was not calibrated to kill deadly germs. Dispirited workers on minimum wage, supplied by temp agencies, donned their uniforms at home, potentially dragging contaminants into the plant, which also had rodents."[3] It's enough to make you want to skip the peanut butter.

How do you make sure this doesn't happen in your company?

How Engaged Are You? The Benefits of Engagement

Employee engagement describes the level of passion and excitement people feel about their work.[4] We often gauge it by the extent to which employees put extra attention, thought, and energy into work, beyond the minimal job requirements. Not acting to repair a leaky roof is "the scream" of a disengaged workforce, and it cost ConAgra more than $66 million in the recall and a sullied reputation. According to Gallup, 16 percent of U.S. workers eighteen and older are "actively disengaged," and the lower productivity of actively disengaged workers costs the U.S. economy about $300 billion.[5]

In stark contrast, highly engaged employees outperform their disengaged colleagues by 20 to 28 percent, according to a study by The Conference Board.[6] Serota Consulting looked at twenty-eight multinational companies and found that the share prices of organizations with highly engaged employees rose by an average of 16 percent, compared with an industry average of 6 percent.[7] The benefits go beyond productivity. Engaged employees are more likely to stay in their jobs, thereby reducing replacement costs. The statistics go on and on.

Has your company engaged and empowered employees enough to act on something as simple as a leaky roof? Wasteful packaging, an inefficient delivery route, or toxic ingredients are all leaks that could jeopardize a company's profitability.

Equally important, *how engaged are the managers?* Does anyone care about those managers as people? In keeping with our call for transparency, another question is, can people handle the truth? Does the company's overarching long-term mission truly engage employees, such that each step toward it is exciting, the next step is clear, and managers know what their employees need to do? Or, are they sitting heads down, focused on the numbers, driven by fear, and disconnected from the staff's needs and the organization's larger purpose? Disengaged leaders might as well be leaky roofs that foster emotional toxicity in the workplace.

Gallup has developed a survey for employees to gauge whether a company succeeds in engaging its workforce. Its questions include the following:

- Do you know what your manager and colleagues expect of you at work?

- Do you have the opportunity to do what you do best every day there?

- Does your supervisor, or someone else at work, seem to care about you as a person?

- Does the mission or purpose of your company make you feel that your job is important?

- Do you have a best friend at work?

- In the last year, did you have an opportunity at work to learn and grow?[8]

What would happen if you took the test? Or if one of your colleagues took it? Do you know what he or she would say?

But Where to Start? Some Positive Psychology

In the past, one approach to coping as a manager and engaging employees was preventing or minimizing the four Ds, that is, damage, disease, disorder, and dysfunction. That brings us back to the peanut butter factory. A leaky roof is a sign of a disengaged workforce, yet managers have historically dealt with problems like the roof as a compliance issue, pressing employees to complete checklists and clean the plant for potential inspections—all earmarks of disengaged management.

Compelling people to comply with the rules at work is the lowest level of engagement. Compliance training means that you are focusing employees on preventing harm instead of promoting good in everything they do at work. As we explained in chapter 4, the problem with compliance is that it often manifests as complacency for producing routine reports on environmental sustainability, and computers can do that better than human beings. Compliance implies that a company is meeting base standards, not raising the bar for competitors and certainly not improving the lives of customers, let alone employees or shareholders. There is a profound difference between avoiding the bad and driving toward the good.

Not surprisingly, engagement is broader than just an employee's job satisfaction; the challenge is to engage the person's entire self and entire psychology. One branch of the field—positive psychology—focuses on just this perspective: creating positive, proactive interventions to make people happy.[9] The pursuit of happiness is not new. It lies at the heart of Aristotle's questions and is embedded in the U.S. Constitution.

Researchers in the field took this philosophical topic and applied clinical research techniques, trying to reverse-engineer what actually makes people happy. They found that once basic material needs like food, water, shelter, safety, and security are met, there are, quite simply, four factors that can help increase one's happiness:

1. Being of service to something larger than yourself

2. Experiencing "flow," or full engagement, on a regular basis

3. Showing your gratitude to the people in your life

4. Sharing your life with at least three close friends or family members[10]

The results of happiness in terms of job effectiveness are stunning. Happier workers have higher incomes, are better organizational citizens, have strong social relationships, and are healthier (both physically and mentally).[11] In "So, How Happy Are You and Your Employees?" you can find ways to evaluate some basic measures of happiness.

Some of the factors listed in "So, How Happy Are You and Your Employees?" may seem difficult to facilitate through the workplace. After all, helping people get married is not exactly the typical job of an employer. But think of the list as a set of positive outcomes to influence the conditions set up at work. A company does not need to get people married, but it should think about how it helps people stay in happy marriages. A company should not require people to be religious, but if they are, then the work environment should support their freedom of religion (while supporting those who are not religious). Later in this chapter, we will explore personal sustainability projects as a mechanism for fostering happiness and driving corporate sustainability.

So, How Happy Are You and Your Employees?

THESE ENGAGEMENT CONCEPTS, while deeply supported by clinical research, are still relatively new to the corporate world. Big businesses worry about becoming too involved in their employees' lives. But people do not have two bodies, two stomachs, two mouths, or two hearts. They are the same person inside and outside the workplace, and building congruence between work life and home life is the key to having an engaged workforce.

The classic measure of this congruence is the Satisfaction with Life Survey, which you can take yourself. Here is an adapted version of the survey:

Rank your agreement with the following statements on a scale of one to seven, where

7 = Strongly agree

6 = Agree

5 = Slightly agree

4 = Neither agree nor disagree

3 = Slightly disagree

2 = Disagree

1 = Strongly disagree

_____ In most ways, my life is close to my ideal.

_____ The conditions of my life are excellent.

_____ I am satisfied with my life.

_____ So far, I have gotten the important things I want in life.

_____ If I could live my life over, I would change almost nothing.

Now, add up all your rankings, to get a total score. Scoring:

35–31 = Extremely satisfied
26–30 = Satisfied
21–25 = Slightly satisfied
20   = Neutral
15–19   = Slightly dissatisfied
10–14   = Dissatisfied
5–9   = Extremely dissatisfied[a]

Where do you think your employees would be on the survey—and what is your responsibility to influence this? Once you know where you and your employees stand, what do you do about it? From the clinical research, Chris Peterson, professor of psychology at the University of Michigan, has compiled a list of contributors to happiness:

- Number of friends

- Being married

- Being extraverted

- Being grateful

- Being religious

- Pursuing leisure activities

- Employment (not income)[b]

a. Adapted in part from William Pavot and Ed Diener, "Review of the Satisfaction with Life Scale," *Psychological Assessment* 5, no. 2 (1993): 164–172, www.psych.uiuc.edu/~ediener/hottopic/pavotDiener1993.pdf.

b. Being employed and making over the equivalent of ten thousand dollars a year is connected to happiness. Any absolute increase in income over that amount has not been correlated directly to happiness. Income does correlate to unhappiness if your peers make more money than you do. In this case, it does not matter how much money you make—if all your friends make more, then chances are, you'll be unhappy.

A Virtuous Cycle: Sustainability Fosters Engagement, Which Fosters Sustainability

Building a long-lasting business with an overarching sustainability goal can provide a greater purpose beyond profits. It can give employees an opportunity to serve something larger than themselves and expose leaky roofs before they become Katrina-sized catastrophes.

Sustainability provides a fresh conversation for soliciting employee input, unleashing employee creativity, surfacing and recognizing leadership talent, and driving innovation—all of which further engage employees. Chances are, your shipping crew or warehouse front line can figure out how to reduce packaging costs. Or a truck driver can recommend how to save gas or cut other transportation costs. Or an administrative assistant can advise you on cutting printing, postage, paperwork, or office maintenance and management costs. Or a cashier can help figure out how to bag a watermelon more cost-effectively.

On one trip to a retail store, I asked a cashier what she thought about bagging watermelons. Her answer was simple. "Well, it sucks," she said. "It takes a long time, wastes a lot of bags, and I bang up my fingers pretty good." How long? "Up to five minutes if I cannot convince the customer to just put it into their cart." She chuckled, "Once, this younger lady insisted I wrap up this huge watermelon. It must have been twenty-five pounds. It took me about ten bags to get it done."

Have you ever seen a cashier try to use small plastic bags to bag a large watermelon? One bag is too few. Double bagging does not work, because the handles are not long enough to hold. You could tie two bags onto each of the handles to expand past the watermelon so that you can carry it in one hand. I made some notes and began to move on to another part of the store, when she stopped me. "Aren't you going to ask me what to do about it?" she asked. "Just put a strap on them." Simple, fast, and environmentally friendlier than ten bags.

The best ideas come from where real social, economic, environmental, and cultural problems are actually solved, which is not necessarily at the top. Engaging a workforce in a strategy for sustainability is an innovation strategy. In its Global Innovation Metrics Survey, McKinsey found the most common metrics that leading companies use to track innovation:

1. Revenue growth due to new products or services (16 percent)

2. Customer satisfaction with new products and services (13 percent)

3. Number of ideas or concepts in the pipeline (10 percent)

4. R&D spending as a percentage of sales (8 percent)

5. Percentage of sales from new products or services in a given period (8 percent)

6. Number of new products or services launched (8 percent)[12]

An effective engagement effort can fuel items 2 and 3 directly. Additionally, enabling people to pursue their passions relative to the company's North Star goal can shorten the length of time between a new product concept and a go-forward decision, ideally to less than three months. Few organizations involve more than 25 percent of their staff in an innovation project. If you effectively organize your engagement effort around your sustainability goal, then you can have near 100 percent participation.

But Will a Strategy for Sustainability Truly Engage Employees?

Yes, people become engaged when their workplace activities connect to what matters in their lives and what makes them happy. And yes, most people want to work at a company with a purpose that goes beyond the next quarter's earnings and that is larger than themselves and the organization. But when the rubber meets the road, will employees actually care about sustainability—as I have defined it, in social, economic, environmental, and cultural terms—enough to engage in corporate efforts to achieve it, and will that make them happier?

I explored a similar question for Walmart, to find out what its associates thought about the environment. We already knew that people born after the first Earth Day in 1970 in the United States received environmental education in grade school and that environmental issues consistently rank as one of the highest concerns of the generation called millennial, the eighty million people born between 1980 and 1995 in the United States. But would Walmart associates in this generation and their older coworkers care enough to engage in Walmart's strategy for sustainability?[13]

We started by interviewing associates in Broomfield, Colorado; Plainfield, Indiana; and Tampa, Florida. We spent days with them in their stores, their communities, and their homes. We talked about what mattered most to them and their families, and we shared the basic concepts behind sustainability. We learned a great deal about the large majority of Walmart associates:

1. *They believe the environment is in crisis.* Once you remove the politics from the equation, people were ready to believe in global warming. They were just not willing to have a political lobotomy—to give up their strongly held political beliefs—to do it.

2. *They want to do something about it.* They lead busy lives with complex demands from family, work, religion, and hobbies. But if they could do something that would also help them achieve their other goals, they were all for it.

3. *They want to learn more about it.* Walmart associates value learning, and any time they had the chance to learn something new that they could share, they were excited. Any time we presented an expert who made them feel dumb, they rebelled.

4. *They have not made sustainability their top priority.* Sustainability does not work as another "thing" to care or worry about. In presenting sustainability as a framework that could help people manage the other priorities in their lives, from personal health to finances, we were able to make it seem a matter of common sense.

Just as sustainability does not work for businesses unless it serves business needs first, sustainability does not engage individuals unless it first and foremost solves problems they experience in their lives. A strategy for sustainability can provide a strong sense of purpose and greater meaning to the company's mission, can connect people to their own job goals, and can speak to the next generation of workers. But it cannot be bolted on: just as it is core to your strategy, it must be integral to their lives. And so, to execute a strategy for sustainability, you must engage individuals personally.

Personal Sustainability Project: How *I* and *My* Family Add Up to *We* and *the World*

To engage the two million associates who work at Walmart, we introduced the Personal Sustainability Project.[14] We hypothesized that if we could learn how to help individuals become personally sustainable, then we might also learn how to affect the two hundred million people who shop regularly at Walmart in America. Now *that*, my friend, is scale.

Some people are more inner directed, and some are more outer directed. Inner-directed people look inside themselves for guidance and serve their own needs first. Outer-directed people look to other people for reinforcement and serve others first. Some people balance both approaches. Sustainability has traditionally existed in the realm of outer-directed people, as a means for them to serve something larger than themselves. By adding the word *personal* to sustainability, we invited everyone to serve.

We started with what has proved to be a great tool of sustainability—small actions anytime, anywhere, that are good for the actors, good for their organization, and good for our planet. It can be as simple as preparing a family dinner once a week, serving vegetables and turning off the TV, and giving thanks for the miracle of your food. Instead of overhauling someone's lifestyle, we started by finding daily or recurring practices that can express an individual's values. We presented it as a simple voluntary commitment called a *personal sustainability practice*, or PSP for short.

What are the qualities of a PSP? It is *repeatable, inspirational, sustainable*, and *enjoyable* (RISE). At its most basic level, it is a healthy habit. People learn to spot PSPs through self-reflection or through a group session where they can talk about their routines and identify changes they would like to make.

We designed the Personal Sustainability Project so that people could recognize, celebrate, and reinforce these achievements at work. For people who wanted to be more connected, we created "idea groups," which they formed around their own PSPs, from healthy eating to energy conservation. The idea groups allowed the participants to meet new people within Walmart. For people who sought leisure activities, for example, the project allowed them to swap stories about, say, gardening, which gave them a sense of status among their peers.

The pioneer associates who developed the project within Walmart began choosing their own unique PSPs and asking their friends and family members to do so as well. They became PSP evangelists. Here are some examples of their personal sustainability practices:

1. Turn the faucet off while brushing your teeth, thereby conserving a natural resource—water (environment)—and reducing your monthly utility bill (economic).

2. Skip a fast-food meal once a week and prepare one at home instead, thereby reducing saturated fat and sodium in your diet (social) and the packaging—the paper-wrapped burger; cardboard container for fries; plastics for lids, straws, and

ketchup; and oh so many napkins—that ends up in a landfill (environmental). If you typically idle your vehicle in the drive-through lane, then skipping a fast-food meal could cut your fuel costs (economic). Perpetuate your family's recipes (cultural).

3. Bike to work, thereby reducing CO_2 emissions (environmental), getting a great workout (social), and potentially cutting health-care costs and health-club fees (economic). Or at least park in the spot farthest from the entrance of the workplace to get some daily exercise. See your neighborhood in a whole new way (cultural).

4. Change lights bulbs to highly efficient CFLs (compact fluorescent lights) or LEDs (light-emitting diodes) to reduce electric bills (economic) and slow global warming (environmental).

5. Care for a nearby park, thereby preserving outdoor play space for children in the community (social, cultural).

We held day-long workshops for hourly associates and store managers from every store, about seventy-five total per event from every market, in each state of the United States. With sustainability knowledge, grassroots enrollment techniques, and a whole lot of inspiration, they went back to their stores and shared the idea with the other associates stores across America.

On the organizational level, we learned that a successful Personal Sustainability Project must have three qualities:

1. *Voluntary*—The project cannot be something that you demand that people do. You simply cannot force people to care about either themselves as individuals, their communities, or the planet. You can, however, touch their hearts and minds and inspire them.

2. *Personal*—It must be connected to the things that matter most—any engagement project must be relevant to daily life. If you have any hope of connecting to a hardworking mom

and dad with kids who need food, clothing, education, and so much more, you must make sustainability relevant on a basic, personal level, rather than on the plane of national parks and planetary impact.

3. *Viral*—The project relies on word of mouth to spread ideas and best personal practices from associate to associate. To succeed, you cannot control how people communicate with each other. At the end of the day, who cares how people are describing their project? What matters is their talking with enthusiasm and purpose—period.

The associates formed teams and store plans, and soon there were ten sustainability captains in every Walmart store, each captain working with the roughly five hundred associates inside to manifest their goals and vision. This grassroots-driven, voluntary movement spread to over forty-five hundred Walmarts and Sam's Clubs across America in the period of about six months. Over half a million Walmart associates (roughly equivalent to the population of Boston) adopted and maintained a PSP in the first year of the project. Interestingly, more than half chose PSPs related to health and wellness, which means that over one-quarter million men and women came through the doors of sustainability because of their own physical health. Or perhaps they developed a stronger interest in their physical health once the Personal Sustainability Project framed sustainability as bigger than their own individual lives— the idea that a concern for the planet implied and required a concern for the individual.

The ideal workplace engagement effort goes far beyond the workplace. Take, for example, the case of Amanda Adler. Amanda is eleven years old and loves to play softball. She lives in Battleground, Washington, a town with a population of about thirteen thousand.[15]

Amanda Adler's mom, Ruth, works at Walmart in Vancouver, Washington. As Ruth got more and more excited about the Personal Sustainability Project and what she could do, Amanda started getting curious and created her own PSP: recycling.

One day in school, Amanda was finishing up drinking out of a plastic bottle and went to put it in her backpack to recycle it. As she did, her teacher asked her what she was doing.

"I'm recycling this," Amanda said.

"Throw it away, Amanda," he said.

"No, I'm recycling this, because that's my PSP."

The teacher was so infuriated that he sent her to the principal's office, where she got detention. When Ruth heard about the incident, she could not believe it. Amanda was a straight-A student; Amanda did not get detention.

Ruth and Amanda decided to do something about it. They set up some chairs on their lawn and waited for the mayor, who happened to live down the block and who walked his dog every evening by their house. When he walked past, they called out to him and invited him over for a chat. He agreed to help.

The mayor had lunch with the superintendent of schools the next day. Within a week, they had recycling programs at the two middle schools and the high school in the community. And they dropped Amanda's detention.

Not surprisingly, the Adlers are just getting started. At dinner, they make sure that there's no TV, and they use it as family time. At the softball league, they got rid of the deep fryer and are now serving up organic vegetables.

Ruth said, "I started in Battleground, and I'm going to Vancouver next." Vancouver has a population of 158,000.[16] I can only imagine what's next.

Small Steps for Engaging Employees in the Workplace

Using the pioneering research of psychologists from Abraham Maslow to Martin Seligman, we've designed a positive framework for focusing engagement efforts at work. To begin, consider the model prepared by Wilmar Schaufeli and his colleagues of the three qualities of engagement at work

- *Vigor*—"high levels of energy and mental resilience while working, the willingness to invest effort in one's work, and persistence even in the face of difficulties."

- *Dedication*—"being strongly involved in one's work and experiencing a sense of significance, enthusiasm, inspiration, pride, and challenge."

- *Absorption*—"being fully concentrated and happily engrossed in one's work, whereby time passes quickly and one has difficulties with detaching oneself from work."[17]

These three qualities provide a lens to consider strategic decisions as well as everyday actions.

How would you describe your own staff? You can tell quickly whether an engagement effort is working. If people are responding equally to meeting requests, volunteering without asking, stretching the program into new directions, and emerging as leaders, then you are succeeding. If it feels like pulling teeth, if people are showing up because they fear skipping it, if you are assigning all the new opportunities to the newest members of your staff without giving your older members a chance, if your social events are about as fun as an IRS audit, then you should probably step back and start over.

British Sky Broadcasting Group plc (BSkyB), one of the leading satellite television providers in the world, with over ten million household subscribers in Britain, has backed up its public commitments to reducing its climate impact by creatively involving its employees. BSkyB has negotiated discounts for employees to purchase hybrids and has given each employee a £1,300 subsidy toward buying a hybrid.[18] It has an innovative game that allows each employee to visualize the "points" that he or she is earning for the employee's environmental efforts. The game starts out as a coral reef, fishless and denuded. Every time an employee commits to, or takes an action for, the environment, a fish enters the reef and something begins to grow. In a very visual sense, the employees see the difference that they're making. The company's programs have worked. In 2006, BSkyB became the first carbon-neutral media company, and it's just getting started.

Steps Toward Successful Engagement, Traps to Avoid

SOMETIMES YOU MIGHT ACCEPT the idea of engaging others toward sustainability, but in practice, you might not know where to start. What follows are descriptions of specific steps you can take, and traps you should avoid, on your way to encouraging others.

FIVE STEPS FOR SUCCESSFUL ENGAGEMENT

1. *Start with your own leadership passion.* Simply put, people follow leaders who have a passion that guides others. Sustainability develops leaders who

    *   understand how to deal with a changing world and market,

    *   approach outside resources and seek their involvement,

    *   reach across organizational silos to find and implement solutions, and

    *   can coordinate and cross-manage finance and communications issues.

    Passion and the ability to share it are keys to sustainability leadership. The managers and team leaders you recruit should have two qualities—a passion for sustainability and a natural aptitude for communication.

Regardless of their technical ability or rank, people who are popular among their peers are some of the most effective leaders of sustainability efforts. Combating organizational inertia is one of the greatest challenges for any sustainability initiative, and the ability to inspire people through passion in a way that involves no blame or judgment allows the possibility for success. If your leadership style is to prove to everyone else how much more you know than they do then you need to look deep into yourself to see if an attitude change is possible.

2. *Tell your own stories.* Start your conversations by telling people what got you started, what you're happy about, or what you love. Share your stories and invite others to share their own; ask how they became interested in sustainability and what it means to them. Good stories have specifics and drama. So ask them hard questions about how their efforts fit into their home life, their family, their everyday worries.

3. *Challenge yourself to go long.* The best North Star goals and PSPs are long-term and not just episodic. Picking up trash once at the beach is good, but it's not a practice unless it's something that you do regularly to improve your life, your community, and the planet. Practices, like sports, yoga, or playing the piano, steady the mind by providing a consistent structure that allows you to excel. Remember to think across social, economic, environmental, and cultural impacts.

4. *Support early adopters and latecomers.* Be on the lookout for your early adopters. They will teach you so much about how the project will work and will probably become your leadership for far beyond your first phase. What engages them? How does it solve their

problems? Make sure that most of your early adopters are not executives, since executives do not generally represent the entire employee population. *Equally important, do not discount your late bloomers, perhaps those with longer tenure, who take longer to understand new technologies and new opportunities, but who embrace them fully and can provide deeper institutional insights for driving them forward.*

5. *Stay positive.* There will always be people who say that your Personal Sustainability Project is impossible. They'll want to argue with you and bring you down. Ignore them. That's their process for creating connection. Stay your course. Your job is not to massage your ego or theirs, but to listen and to serve, which means getting the most people possible engaged in the larger project. If people want to participate, then let them— but regularly check in with them on their workload.

TRAPS TO AVOID

In the end, building a sustainability engagement effort is not rocket science. The big question is, Does this serve the audience? Here are four traps that companies get stuck in when they make this effort:

1. *Preaching*—Everyone will decide for himself or herself. The best you can do is to present to the people the world as you see it, in a way that's digestible to them, and then show them a path to take. Focusing too much on your own gospel is a good way to ensure that few others will be joining you on the path.

2. *Using scary facts without the good news*—Sure, there are scary facts, and we should not avoid them. But unless you share with people the sense of possibility and opportunity, they are likely to shut down. Bad

news is hard to bear, and sometimes letting the bad news sink in without hard-selling it enables people to feel as if they have a choice about how to respond.

3. *Evoking authority*—"You have to do this because an eminent scientist said so." If you yourself cannot convince people by how you listen to, learn from, and respond to their needs, do not expect that quoting important scientists, politicians, or celebrities will effect change. You must connect with people and inspire a sense of possibility. When you invoke distant authority, you have lost your audience.

4. *Not giving people a place to start*—The worst thing you can do is to get people excited about the power they have and then leave them without anything to do with that power—or, worse, excluding them from exciting efforts under way because "so-and-so is already on that committee." They will leave the experience feeling dejected and used. Always have a few options for what they can do today.

Many Small Steps Can Add Up to One Giant Leap: Tackling Health Care

During the Internet bubble, businesses were focused on the "killer app," the software application that would drive users to their Web site and thereby slay the competition. In the short term, the killer app for sustainability might be the savings in energy use that a company can find by looking. After all, saving money and increasing productivity is easy to measure and value. But in the years to come, people will increasingly use the sustainability tool set to maintain their health. Connecting how you treat your body and the higher purpose of sustainability is the killer app. From losing weight to exercising, eating more unpackaged fruits and vegetables, and quitting cigarettes, sustainability enables people to experience self-efficacy, whether by lowering their energy bill by switching off the lights, or by feeling a sense of accomplishment by helping to restore a wetland. Success begets success and creates a positive reinforcement loop that will influence your business work environment.

We began working with the largest health benefits company (in terms of medical membership) in the United States—WellPoint—to integrate sustainability into the health-care sphere. Through its affiliated health plans, WellPoint serves thirty-five million members across the country, or one in nine Americans.

Today, WellPoint is trying to move the health-care industry away from disease management and toward "health production." Its goal is to engage the people it insures to be health partners—helping them to lead healthier lives. WellPoint resolved that in order to really impact health engagement in the marketplace, it needed to first engage its own associates with personal sustainability. Day in and day out, WellPoint associates are there to help customers engage in their own health care by answering questions about benefits, reminding customers to take their medication, by answering questions about diets, and coaching them into healthier lifestyles.

While these WellPoint associates feel passionate about the services they deliver to their customers, many struggle to find their own way to thrive and be healthy. WellPoint offers its associates a range of wellness programs, from prevention and condition care to physical activity, nutrition, weight management, and tobacco cessation. Many associates take advantage of these programs and realize the benefits that come from losing weight or quitting smoking, but struggle to fit wellness into their busy lives. The challenge for the people who work at WellPoint is to get them to live the lives that they wish for their members. Or, "Physician, heal thyself," in biblical words.

Working with Joan Kennedy, president of Health Management Corporation (HMC), a subsidiary of WellPoint responsible for helping to improve the health of employees at companies across the United States, we are exploring how PSP can help drive health engagement with WellPoint's employees and members. A pilot

Personal Sustainability Project for WellPoint associates was launched in September 2008. WellPoint's PSP is designed to complement its existing wellness programs, introducing sustainability as an additional means for associates to take personal action and accountability for their health and wellness.

Joan Kennedy's grandfather, Henry Swan, was one of the founders of open-heart surgery. During one of our conversations, Joan explained that her original career path was centered on international service work. But inspired by her grandfather's work, she decided to pursue a profession that would allow her to preserve the world by preventing the very types of surgeries her grandfather performed. "I see my mission as helping health plans to take accessing health care to a higher level by providing members with products and services that help keep them well," she said.

Joan endorses the idea of personal sustainability practices because she believes the key to helping people live healthier lives is taking one step at a time. "We are bombarded by messages that tell us the many things we should be doing to improve ourselves: lose fifty pounds, eat more vegetables, exercise for twenty minutes daily." Her voice rises as she speaks more quickly. "But, if people can feel good about the one small step they take, they will develop the self-esteem and confidence needed to move to the next step."[19]

As WellPoint takes strides toward becoming a sustainable organization and focuses on leading the health-care industry with a sustainable product offering, we may finally begin to see progress in halting and, hopefully, reversing some of the most frightening trends this country faces in health care.

Diabetes, heart disease, hypertension, and childhood obesity are just a few conditions that are totally preventable with proper nutrition and exercise. Perhaps the efforts to stop climate change and create sustainable business operations may also be the thing to save millions of lives. Or, as Brad Perkins, chief strategy and innovation officer of the Centers for Disease Control and Prevention, said metaphorically about the health-care system, "We need to stop simply lining up ambulances for wrecks at the bottom of the cliff, and start building guard rails at the top—protecting health so we have less disease."[20] Perkins helped lead the CDC's response to the anthrax threat in the United States after 9/11, but his passion as a public health professional is to extend life expectancy by preventing disease before it happens.

Two thousand years ago every Chinese village had a doctor. That doctor was paid by the people who were in good health and he treated the people in bad health free of charge. This payment method was a good incentive for the doctor to keep everyone healthy, to prevent disease rather than treat it later. Getting the structural incentives right is critical, but there is a lot people can do right now to improve their own quality of life. The first step is making the choice to do something.

Act Now: Choose Your Own PSP

As a leader, you make a difference with your own actions. Here are some steps you can take to start your own Personal Sustainability Practice:

- Review and reflect on your responses to the basic Gallup poll questions and happiness questions discussed in this chapter.

- Identify an area that enhances your life, for example, friends, family, and being in nature.

- Think of a personal sustainability practice that would improve your day, even in the smallest way.

- Ask yourself, is it repeatable, inspirational, sustainable, and enjoyable?

- Start small, start now, and share what you are doing with peers, family, and friends.

- Ask the people closest to you in your life to develop their own PSPs. Recall that a core quality of engaged employees is that they have an engaged manager and an engaged support system.

- Commit to it publicly, and start sharing stories of setbacks and successes.

CHAPTER SIX

The Network of Sustainability Partners

A Company Cannot Execute Its Strategy Alone

WHEN I WAS eight years old, my parents received a petition to oust James G. Watt, the secretary of the interior under President Ronald Reagan. Watt wanted to privatize parts of the U.S. national park system. I did not know who Watt was, I certainly did not know what *privatization* meant, but I did know how to sign my name; I had just learned how to do that in school. So I brought the petition to my class's show-and-tell, and all my friends signed it with those fat second-grade pencils. Because of my enthusiasm or stubbornness, my teacher let me walk through the school and get other kids to sign. Pretty soon, I had a hundred signatures, and those signatures joined a million more. Watt lost his job. I had become an activist.

In high school, I recruited thirty thousand students across the United States to form the Sierra Student Coalition with the North Star goal to protect the last wilderness left in the United States. And in 1994, we helped create Death Valley National Park, the largest national park in the lower forty-eight states.[1] The coalition was a loose network of activists across the country, and we grew effective by letting the local groups keep their own identity and by helping them share their campaign ideas across the network. Students in Georgia launched a corporate campaign against Shell to protest its treatment of the Ogoni tribe in Nigeria. Other students in Rhode Island launched campus boycotts of Nike gear at university shops to respond to its use of sweatshops. We used the World Wide Web, which in 1994 was still mostly confined to universities and military institutions (eBay wasn't founded until 1995), to share these campaign ideas around the network, and the campaigns spread like wildfire.

When I graduated from college, I staged a minicoup with the help of some wily older activists and was elected president of the Sierra Club, the largest grassroots environmental group in the United States. Founded in 1892, the Sierra Club had, and still has, the North Star goal to explore, enjoy, and protect the natural and human environment. The organization has been protecting land since its founder, John Muir, convinced President Teddy Roosevelt to protect Yosemite. What Muir knew, and what I learned back as an eight-year-old, is that anyone, no matter how inexperienced or lacking in rank, can contribute to effect change greater than oneself. And you can rally large groups of individuals around a common cause—a North Star goal—and effect even greater change in existing institutions. Once you've got empowered people with a North Star goal, you can network organizations with similar North Stars—like Sierra Club and Greenpeace—around those same goals, and the results can be exponential. But the network of environmental organizations, even linked together, still wasn't large enough to tackle climate change. By that time, I was convinced of the urgency of responding to climate change and I knew it wasn't going to happen by civic activism alone. So in 1998, I left the Sierra Club to found my own company, Act Now, so that I could try to engage the very people against whom I had been protesting for all those years. You risk being called a sellout if you have roots in the activist community and attempt to aid companies in transformation.[2] But that's a small price to pay for breaking with conventional orthodoxies in service of a larger goal.

How big is the goal? It spans the entire sustainability continuum—social, economic, environmental, and cultural. Our society has three billion people who regularly don't have clean water. The global economy needs twenty-first-century rules and institutions. Our natural environment faces catastrophic climate change, and our individual cultures are becoming more homogenized each year. We need to replumb every village, rewire every house, revisit Breton Woods, and increase our cultural diversity each year.

Big challenges require big solutions. Fighting off a global recession takes trillions of dollars of investment. Even slowing climate change requires that we lower our carbon emissions by 80 percent by 2050. No single community, company, activist group, or country can do it alone. And that's why network organizing is inevitable as a means of achieving great goals.

Just changing how a company makes products or delivers a service requires instigators like you to use your network differently. To do so, you must decide on many issues:

- Which problems to share

- How to connect them to a North Star goal, so as to identify outsiders who can help or are part of the problem

- How to bring in outsiders

- How to educate and learn from an apparent enemy

- How to exercise leadership through policy

This chapter addresses those issues.

Amazon McNuggets

In the spring of 2006, McDonald's awoke to a public relations nightmare. Posters of Ronald McDonald wielding a chainsaw were plastered in McDonald's restaurants across Britain, and dozens of Greenpeace activists were dressed as seven-foot-tall chickens and chained to chairs in McDonald's European restaurants.[3] Greenpeace activists had traced the soybeans used in feed of the chickens used in Chicken McNuggets to the rapid destruction of the Amazon rain forest.[4] Three years into a turnaround strategy that was driving more consumers into their restaurants, McDonald's didn't need a crisis to chase them away. In this case, the network itself chose the problem, and McDonald's needed to decide whether to put up the barricades and send out the lawyers or to let the drawbridge down and start learning.

To understand how McDonald's found itself in this situation, we need to flash back to the 1980s. The soybean crop arrived in Brazil and took off like poppies used for heroin. A decade into the soy addiction in 1992, Greenpeace opened an office deep in the rain forest and began mapping wherever human activity was destroying the forest. Deforestation contributes to 20 percent of climate change.[5] At first, Greenpeace tracked illegal logging, then cattle ranching, and then soy harvesting. As the commodity markets changed, the threats to the forest changed as well. Noticing an uptick in illegal logging for soy plantations, Greenpeace used an airplane with global positioning system (GPS) mapping to scout the extent of the destruction. The organization then conducted a meticulous chain-of-custody study to determine who was buying and who was using the illegally harvested soy. Its study uncovered logging in illegal areas, soy farming on public land (a crime), and even slave labor on some farms.

But despite Greenpeace's effort, the forests have suffered. Thanks to low land prices and a highly lucrative animal feed industry, over seventy thousand square kilometers of the Amazon forest have been logged since 2003. According to Greenpeace, Brazil is now the world's fourth-largest emitter of CO_2 on the planet, and 75 percent of Brazil's emissions comes from deforestation, which occurs mostly in the Amazon.[6]

From 2004 to 2006, the global demand for soy rocketed. Farmers made less than $200 per hectare with cattle, but could make up to $1,200 per hectare with soy. Representing 10 percent of Brazilian exports, the soy trade brings in about $30 billion a year. Most of the trade involves a few companies—Cargill, ADM, and Bungee—that traffic the crop for animal feed, cooking oil, and biofuel. The demands of society—more specifically, those of the 21 percent of Brazilians who live on less than $2 a day, combined with those of wealthier consumers and industries—pushed soy farmers deeper into the forest.[7] New technologies allowed soy to be used more commonly in everyday products. And rising costs of natural resources, namely, oil, encouraged the use of soy as an alternative fuel source.

Greenpeace tracked Cargill's Amazon soybeans to Liverpool, where the British chicken producer Sun Valley fed the soy to the chickens used in McNuggets in Europe. McDonald's response to this supply-chain sustainability crisis is a case study in what every organization can do to engage its suppliers and the nonprofit community in finding a solution.

As a member of the international board of Greenpeace, I went on a fact-finding mission to the Amazon to understand what was happening. There, I met Ivete, an earnest leader of a local workers cooperative who is under constant federal protection due to threats on her life. (I've omitted her name for safety reasons.) Ivete lives near San Pedro not far from the confluence of the Amazon and the Tapajos Rivers, where the cutting was occurring. She spoke rapidly, her hands gesticulating, "We face some serious challenges here . . . After Cargill came in 2003, we faced huge pressure to sell our lands."

Of the families working the area, 90 percent do not have official title to their lands, and many have been kicked off. The government has been slow at land reform and at settling the disputes. "The big landowners get their papers first," Ivete said, "even though the new constitution gave us our land."

Soon after the large landowners received their papers, the police came and told many of the smaller landowners that the land was not theirs. Some entire communities disappeared. "The process was violent," she said, shaking her head. "There have been fifteen hundred thirty-four workers assassinated in the last fifteen years."

In one town, Genipapo, there were forty-five families with a new church and a new water system. They were almost finished with a rural electrification project when a farmer named Casagrand (which translates roughly to "big house") claimed that all this land was his and led efforts to frighten them from their homes. When I arrived, the smell of smoke was still fresh. I saw the charred remains of the houses whose owners had resisted. The school had closed, and the remaining twelve families were struggling to stay. The local government was controlled by the big landowners like Casagrand and turned a blind eye to the wreckage. I still carry some soybeans that I found there to remind me of the social, economic, environmental, and cultural costs that the people of the Amazon are paying for the way we live.

Marcelo Furtado, executive director of Greenpeace Brazil, explained why the activists chose to go after Cargill first: "They were the largest and a fast-growing buyer of soy from the forest, and they already had a strained relationship with the community. Before we started, they showed an unwillingness to meet."[8] Once Furtado and the Greenpeace team were ready to release the report connecting Cargill to illegal activities, he flew to Washington, D.C., to give the company one last chance to change, but Cargill's management team refused.

So Greenpeace targeted the next big global brand further down the supply chain: McDonald's. Contrary to the advice of those public relations consultants who coach corporate clients into immediate denials in response to such attacks, McDonald's officials listened carefully and responded openly. "[We] will be investigating the claim made by Greenpeace in full and will review it for consistency in line with our existing policy not to source beef from recently deforested areas," they said.[9] Two points are important here: (1) McDonald's had previously established a policy for supply-chain sustainability, which guided its employees in this situation, and (2) whenever someone uncovers such a problem that McDonald's has contributed to, whether inadvertently or not, McDonald's has committed to contributing to its solution. In this case, once Greenpeace proved that McDonald's was linked to a system that contributed to illegal logging in the Amazon, McDonald's brought Cargill and the other major soy producers of the Amazon together to craft a sustainable solution.

Bob Langert, vice president for corporate social responsibility at McDonald's, told me, "The McDonald's of ten years ago would have reacted differently. Now, we first ask, 'What's going on?'"[10] He told the *Washington Post* at the time, "We listened to what Greenpeace was saying about soy from the rain forest, and I think we surprised them at first by saying, 'you're right. We have a problem here.' We have a firm policy against using beef—or any other products—that come from the rain forest. So when we learned that some of our soy was coming from there, we got involved."[11] According to Greenpeace's Furtado, "After they realized they were implicated, they wanted to know how they could be part of the solution, not the problem."[12]

McDonald's and Greenpeace teamed up. With pressure from Greenpeace, McDonald's ability to collaborate with its suppliers, and both organizations' recruiting like-minded organizations to the effort, Brazil's biggest soy traders placed a two-year moratorium on the purchase of soy from recently deforested areas. Through their work, the illegal cutting was halted as Cargill and other major soy traders enacted a voluntary ban on buying soybeans from newly logged forests. So far, the soy moratorium has protected millions of acres. On McDonald's part, the company avoided a public relations disaster, guaranteed the stability of its Chicken McNuggets supply chain at no increase in price, and did something wonderful for the world. Langert had only good things to say about

Greenpeace: "They didn't dress up like chickens in our meetings. What most people don't realize is how good and thoughtful and professional most NGOs are. I admire them."

Cargill later confirmed the importance of these two unlikely allies. "McDonald's and, yes, Greenpeace, were the catalysts," said Laurie Johnson, a spokeswoman for Cargill. "They brought together a wide range of people and created a sense of real urgency."[13] Langert believes this is just the beginning: "If we can work together smartly and strategically, it's amazing what we can do."

McDonald's was by no means the largest buyer of soy, but because it benefited from the cheap soybeans grown in the supply-chain network, and because of its global visibility, its leaders found themselves held accountable. The challenge for twenty-first-century companies is how to use networks to drive down their costs, increase their accountability, and bring themselves closer to the customer.

Setting Up a Network Structure for Sustainability

Remember that nature works in systems, solves problems in groups, and is transparent. Each part of the system knows its role, and nothing is superfluous.

That's radically different from the way many companies position their sustainability effort. As a general rule (with many exceptions), sustainability efforts that emanate from the public affairs or the legal department don't have the organizational tools to succeed, because those offices rarely initiate future-oriented business decisions. You'll want to position the hub of your network such that a company's primary stakeholders and decision makers can easily see its work and the social, economic, environmental, and cultural results. Once the hub has been established, use the network frequently for problems that the organization regards as important.

The five dimensions of a healthy network

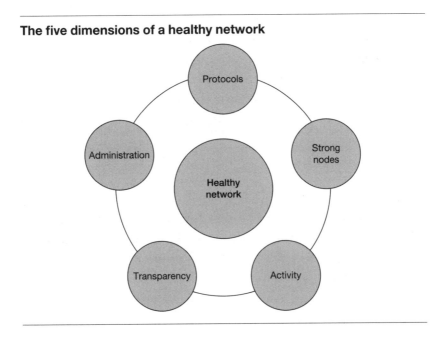

A healthy network has five dimensions:

Protocols—A network cannot function without explicit rules or protocols. If people in your company do not know the rules and incentives for engaging outsiders, then they will shy away from doing so, to avoid doing something wrong. You must form a clear statement of support for outreach and train staff on acceptable outreach practices.

Activity—Networks fail without lots of activity. If you form a network of insiders and outsiders, but gather them annually, they will probably not bring you much value. In social networks, you must rebuild any relationship dormant for more than a month before it will function at its prior level.

Strong nodes—A network is only as strong as the nodes of people who participate. Just asking the advice of any outsider will not help. You must find organizations and individuals with specific experience in, or influence on, your industry, and you must support them with information and access. The currency for many nonprofits is the change they can achieve, and sometimes, the information that you can share, at no cost to you, can help these groups push the entire industry to change.

Transparency—Information fuels networks, and the information will come from your transparency initiatives. Networks use information to solve problems and build relationships. Without information, there is no network.

Administration—A network must have an administrator. Administrators should not dominate the communications, but should play traffic cop. Someone must make sure that joining the network is easy, that queries reach the right person, and that the network's communications technology works.

A network is only as strong as its nodes. Recruit your network captains carefully. Look for natural leaders. For example, I worked with a CEO who believed that all the members of the company's internal leadership development program should participate in the sustainability effort to prove their mettle for long-term reliability. Other companies allow leadership to bubble up to the top. Who's excited by sustainability? Who has experience with successful initiatives in the company? Once you have recruited your network captains, there are five rules that will help them become effective (see "Rules for Your Network Captains").

How to Engage Your Outsiders

In my book, *Act Now, Apologize Later*, I described Walmart as threatening to destroy the environment of the planet and the culture of the United States. So, no one was more puzzled than I when Walmart called me to discuss sustainability. At that time, labor unions were waging a high-profile campaign against Walmart. I knew that simply meeting with Walmart representatives—let

Rules for Your Network Captains

1. **Make connections.** In 1973, American sociologist Mark Granovetter wrote a seminal paper on networking, "The Strength of Weak Ties," in which he shows how a network of many distant connections can be more effective than a network of a few close connections.[a] So if you are looking for a job, you may get better leads from your acquaintances than from your best friends. For a sustainability network leader, keeping a large group of people up-to-date through e-mail, blogging, and social gatherings is critical to find the right solution at the right time. Few companies have the capacity to hire all the intelligence internally—your connections will drive your network.

2. **Celebrate change.** If your sustainability effort is to succeed, then it must drive innovation in your organization and your network. Change does not come easily for successful organizations. If you get stuck, ask people whether they can describe another initiative (not related to sustainability) that was controversial or unexpected at the time, but turned out to be critical to company success. Ask them to describe why it succeeded.

3. **Know your company's top objectives.** Once again, sustainability is a business strategy. If you do not know the three things your board or CEO worries about every day when they wake up, then you're not ready to lead. You will find great leaders to be part of your network if they know the initiative is tied to the company's broader success. I'm amazed when these

top objectives do not roll off the tongues of people working on sustainability initiatives.

4. **Understand that sustainability is a nomadic journey.** I have not yet found a completely sustainable business. Yvon Chouinard, the founder of clothing and equipment maker Patagonia and one of the world's most dedicated sustainability advocates, has said, "Everyone is greenwashing." If you are serious about this work, it will not be over before you retire.

5. **Do something.** Err on the side of action. In every sustainability effort, there will be naysayers and doubters, and there will be supporters who want you to drive the initiative toward their small agenda. So, spend as much time executing change as possible. Early on, find an example of someone in your organization who "broke the rules" to make a sustainability innovation, and celebrate this person's achievement. Perhaps a shipping clerk devised new packaging and skipped over the boss to talk directly to the marketing department. Or maybe an engineer changed the climate controls without authorization, saved the company thousands of dollars, and kept tons of CO_2 from the atmosphere. Encourage action as opposed to analysis, authorization, and measurement. The measurement will come later. Or maybe your company is smaller, and a well-liked assistant or an intern is jamming your inbox full of ideas and staying late to sketch them out. Publicly acknowledge them and give them some space to succeed.

a. Mark S. Granovetter, "The Strength of Weak Ties," *American Journal of Sociology* 78, no. 6 (May 1973): 1360–1380.

alone lunching with them—would raise eyebrows among activists and the media.

"What should I do?" I asked one grizzled activist. Leaning forward in his chair, he growled, "First, you need to understand it's a trap. They're going to try to convince you with their facts, and you have to make sure that you do not give them an inch that they can later use against you." I nodded, not quite knowing how they would use something against me. "Make sure not to let them buy you lunch," he said definitively. "If they buy you lunch, you'll become tainted."

I resolved to have my credit card handy when the check arrived.

Two Walmart vice presidents and I met at Town Hall restaurant in San Francisco. They told me of Walmart's plans to achieve three goals:

1. To produce zero waste

2. To sell products that sustain our resources and environment

3. To run 100 percent on renewable energy

Walmart had not announced these goals publicly, and so I was noticeably stunned and enthusiastic. If Walmart, the retailer with almost two hundred million shoppers annually and two million employees worldwide, was setting what seemed like North Star goals to me, and ones that I shared, then sustainability as I knew it was about to scale.[14] Imagine if only a fraction of these associates spoke to their families, their churches, and their customers about leading lives more sustainable.

The executives peppered me with questions about how to make sustainability attractive to the broadest set of the American public. How to engage their associates. How to measure success. Whom I respected and whom they should be talking to. They spoke candidly about their challenges and called on my expertise in facing them.

When the check arrived, I forgot to cue up my credit card. Not to worry: Walmart never buys anyone lunch.

What struck me about our meal was Walmart's recognition of how my knowledge could serve its system and how I could participate in solving its larger business problems, and so the company opened up its goals to me. Everyone has access to information about a company's abilities and inabilities to face its own global challenges of sustainability—enough information to criticize the company. Conversely, you have access to information about your critics as well as those who already share your North Star goals or whom you can convince to join you. So why not identify, connect with, and open up to the outside expertise that can help you?

How to Educate and Enlist Your Enemies and Other Outsiders

As an activist, you might find it relatively simple to attack a company. Visit a factory undercover, take some photos, write a report, put up a Web site, call the media. Companies make it easy; they overstate their claims, they react defensively, they move slowly, and they rarely listen. Something happens when companies receive outside criticism or enlist their critics. Sometimes it is because the outsider looks or talks differently. Sometimes the timing is just inconvenient. Or sometimes it's nobody's designated responsibility to respond to comments. Whatever the cause, the initial reaction from most companies is to ignore or reject criticism.

Why wouldn't a company have an 800 number on the back of its package to hear about product quality issues? The small additional cost to field comments far outweighs the costs of unhappy customers. Similarly, nonprofit leaders are a supergroup for customer input. These are opinion leaders who can spread their anger quickly through the Internet. But still, most companies lack substantial mechanisms to incorporate these outsiders into their strategy. So how can you tell if they're out to bring you down or just trying to help?

Outside organizations will sometimes approach a company with the only language they know, which can be full of bluster, threats, and judgments. Your first effort must be to listen. Think of McDonald's and Greenpeace.

For years, General Electric was a top target of outside organizations, largely due to its failure to understand the public's concern for environmental protection. The company's stubborn refusal to clean up its toxics in the Hudson River epitomized this arrogance. Today, General Electric sees sustainability as a core part of its growth plan, has taken responsibility for the cleanup of the Hudson, and has engaged outside organizations like the Environmental Defense Fund and Conservation International in its effort. GE's CEO Jeff Immelt comments frequently on how outsiders help GE understand opportunities and liabilities.

Keep in mind that your role as an internal instigator of your company's strategy for sustainability differs from the outside advocate's; don't expect the outsider to step into your shoes. Companies need to decide; it is not the role of an outside organization to do so. Your company lives or dies by the consequences of those decisions. It is not the job of the government or the nongovernment organization to know your business; it is your job. Outside organizations will not come to you as a consultant interested in servicing your needs; their goal is to serve the needs of their own people and causes. It is not their job to help you make more money. But they can help make you smarter.

You need these people to help you question and clarify your own purpose. You should be advocating for your customer and your shareholder. The outsiders should be advocating for their members and their mission. If you've got your STaR map pointed in the right direction, then there might be a lot of overlap.

Some nonprofit leaders choose not to learn. They have their opinions and are inflexible. They have already set their course. That rigidity makes them valuable. If you encounter this sort of advocate, and your goal remains to build a strategy for sustainability into the fiber of your company, learn everything you can from them and move on. The advocate who wants to learn the basics of your business will pay great dividends. Advocate networks are tight, and once you introduce information openly and honestly into the system, it will spread readily. And if you're honest about it, you might find solutions that will help you tackle your issues. In the case of some issues that will only be solved by governments, multi-corporate partnerships, or multinational agreements, involving advocates may be a critical step toward success.

Policy Leadership: Changing the Playing Field

As your sustainability initiative moves out of the exploratory phase and into the leadership phase, you will begin to find areas of leadership in policy that can help your business thrive. Legislators respond favorably to strange collaborations of business and civic groups.

Consider Dell, one of the largest computer retailers on the planet.[15] Dell had been a laggard in responding to environmental issues, at one point telling shareholders that it would get involved in recycling computers as soon as customers wanted them to be recycled. The Silicon Valley Toxics Coalition mocked a Dell ad campaign and started promoting viral ads with the tagline, "Dude, Take Back My Dell." In 2003, when nearly every environmental group converged on Dell as a target, Dell soon created a leading computer take-back program.[16]

"We had been engaged since Dell's inception, but we had our sights set on driving environmental considerations into every aspect of our business," said Tod Arbogast, director of sustainable business at Dell.[17]

For Dell's charismatic founder, Michael Dell, the inspiration came from his daughter. "I've got a 15-year-old daughter, and she cares about these issues," said Dell. "And if she cares about these issues, I care about these issues."[18]

Dell had two strategies. The first is to engage its opponents— namely, the Silicon Valley Toxics Coalition, the Texas Campaign for the Environment, and CERES—and the second is to expand the company's commitment. Dell turned its oppositional relationships with nonprofits into productive partnerships with recycling and waste organizations supporting its computer-take-back programs. Every quarter, Michael Dell holds a meeting with his direct reports to review the progress of Dell's sustainability initiative.

Today, Dell will take back every computer that it makes, at no cost to the consumer. It works with organizations like Goodwill to ensure that the parts are recycled, and when the computers are usable, Dell donates them to deserving families through the National Cristina Foundation.[19] Dell has lobbied alongside its partners for computer-take-back legislation.

Now that Dell has created a supply chain and aptitude for computer recycling, the company's initiative has given it a competitive edge. "From there, we recognized what we knew but we needed help on the legislative front; we needed to encourage greater adoption of producer responsibility," said Arbogast, referencing the laws that require manufacturers to take back Dell equipment.

The take-back program was a profit-making venture for Dell's government and corporate accounts, which account for about 85 percent of the computers that Dell sells. But with other consumers, Dell was losing money by recycling its computers, even though Dell believes that everyone should recycle. "For consumers, we think that as you place products in the marketplace, you must provide no-charge, convenient recycling," said Arbogast.

In this case, Dell was incurring additional cost by doing the right thing. The solution? Level the playing field. Dell's aim is to require the rest of the industry to bear the same costs through legislation. In 2007, Dell started working in the company's home state of Texas along with nongovernmental organizations to pass Texas legislation that mandated recycling for all manufacturers.[20]

"We want to get the whole U.S., and eventually the world, requiring that manufacturers take back their PCs," said Arbogast. "As a result of the hard work of our employees and feedback from customers, partners, and suppliers, we're on our way to becoming a leader."

If your company invests in energy efficiency and low-carbon production before your competitors do, then your business needs strong legislation on climate change. If you can innovate and remove a chemical from your supply chain, then you can lobby for getting that chemical banned. If you can get your employees to use public transportation, then it is in your interest to have government pass commuter legislation that gives tax-free public transportation benefits. If you can get a high percentage of local ingredients, know-how, or labor involved in customizing your products, then you can reap tax benefits. These actions have societal, environmental, cultural, *and* economic benefits. You are helping to change the field in a way that allows your business to compete and win.

You're already leveraging networks; supercharging your investment in your network will drive your strategy for sustainability. As you visualize your sustainability network, imagine it dissolving the four walls of your company. Just as free-trade laws have broken down trade barriers across countries, imagine increasingly transparent companies sharing common problems widely through their networks. Imagine your company relying even more on your suppliers to improve your performance. At our office in San Francisco, one of our staff members chose a personal sustainability practice of drinking fair-trade, shade-grown, organic coffee (referred to as *triple-certified*). Working with our operations team, he took it upon himself to call our coffee vendor and asked the people there about the coffee they were supplying us. As a group, we discussed changing vendors to support a small, sustainable supplier that was triple-certified. How did we decide? We went back to our North Star goal of getting one billion people to choose personal sustainability practices. It was unlikely that this small supplier would quickly get to the scale we needed to start getting better coffee choices to a billion people, and more likely that the larger company would be a better partner to us. The larger company, Berkeley's PEET's coffee, is highly attuned to our North Star goal and is a learning lab for us, with highly motivated employees, a passion for coffee, and a desire to improve the world and grow its business simultaneously. So we stuck with our original vendor, and we're learning more about sourcing coffee than we could have ever expected, which we'll then pass on to the thousands of people we train each year.

Sometimes, the resources are closer than you think. In the next chapter, you'll read about how Xerox is helping businesses across the world run their businesses better and use less paper in the process.

Act Now: Bring Outsiders In

Here are some practical ways you can bring outsiders into your organization. Remember, the point is to use the outsider as a source of new ideas that may not come out of your own corporate mind-set. With this in mind, it is important to view outsiders as helpful, not antagonistic, to your North Star goals.

1. Write a list of the three outside organizations, particularly grassroots organizations that will drive the external agenda for you in the next five years. How many of them do you have relationships with? Subscribe to their e-mail newsletters.

2. Invite them to lunch at a casual restaurant, and listen. Learn about their organization and what they're trying to accomplish. Learn about why they're interested in your company. Ask them about their worldview and the role of business within it. At the first meeting, your entire goal should be to understand the basis of their concerns and to learn about what has influenced their thinking. Do not pretend to listen. It wastes your time and theirs. If the conversation moves quickly into horse-trading, negotiation, or compromise, then you are off track.

3. There is one *litmus test* question you should ask yourself to help decide whether to work with an outside organization,

even if the group is not easy to work with: can it make
us better?

After your initial contact with the outside organization, here are
some suggestions for subsequent meetings:

1. The best way to build camaraderie and partnership with an
   outside group is to travel together to examine the underlying issues. Together you will build common knowledge that
   you can use as a basis for communication.

2. A great "first date" is to take a trip together to the municipal waste station. Even if your company does not produce,
   sell, or distribute any disposable good, it does use products
   that end up in landfills. The amount of waste each of us
   creates every day is a good place to begin the dialogue. The
   San Francisco–based household products company, method,
   takes every new employee to the San Francisco recycling
   facility so that the person gets a sense of what he or she
   is creating.

3. Think about where else you might go. To return to the
   McDonald's and Greenpeace example, a journey (in their
   case, to the Amazon) can bring a great deal of clarity and
   resolve to a cooperative effort. Seeing satellite images of
   clear-cut acres was enough to get the process started. But
   witnessing deforestation firsthand convinced the company
   to put pressure on soy traders and change how business was
   being done.

CHAPTER SEVEN

Leadership at All Levels

Inspiration as a Leadership Technique

JAN BENNETT was not accustomed to sitting in a posh meeting room of an Aspen resort hotel. A far cry from her home in Broomfield, Colorado, the place was filled with the world's eco-intelligentsia like Al Gore and *New York Times* columnist Thomas Friedman. For most of her life, she has worked in retail, living from paycheck to paycheck. Originally from Mississippi, she comes from a long line of women with fried foods as a staple of their diet. She is a lifelong learner and was excited about learning how sustainability works, what exactly is happening to our atmosphere, and how recycling can be a business driver. She had volunteered to become a Personal Sustainability Project captain in Walmart's Broomfield store and soon had engaged almost every associate in the store.

Here she was, a participant in an exclusive, clean-energy invest-ment conference at the Aspen Institute. She wanted to make sure these people fully understood what average Americans think about climate change.

At some point in the proceedings, a high-ranking government official stood up and said climate issues were too complex for aver-age Americans. The implication was that experts rather than aver-age earthlings should be solving the problem.

There he was, dismissing her work to change people's behavior, her encouraging people to replace their light bulbs with ecofriendly ones and turn down their heat. Jan could not hold her tongue. She knew that such experts had been working on climate change for twenty years, with little progress.

She summoned her courage, stood up, and said, "Discount me, and the South will rise up in me; inspire me, and I will move any mountain you put in front of me."[1] This humble hourly worker had just corrected a high-level political appointee, a renowned expert in clean-energy policy. She glanced around. Silence. Oh, dear. Why had Walmart invited her to this conference?

Then Vice President Gore started to clap. Pretty soon, everyone else was applauding Bennett as well.

Bennett epitomizes a fully engaged employee, whose engagement and access to information and talent throughout Walmart's web of resources enabled her to lead a sustainability initiative. She was inspired and inspiring.

In one early conversation, Bennett told me that her new personal sustainability practice was a diet. "Really?" I asked, obviously dis-appointed that this leader had chosen to go with something so . . . ordinary.

"What do you mean, 'Really?'?" she snapped back.

"Well, I just figured that s u s t a i n a b i l i t y"—I said it slowly this time—"has to have something to do with protecting the earth."

Bennett gave me a kind sigh. "Where do you think all that food is coming from?"

She paused. "And what about sustaining me, so I can sustain my family?" She smiled. "You'll figure it out."

I finally understood that her dual goals—learning to recycle and to lose weight—were the touchstone of her transformation. Bennett wanted to lose about seventy-five pounds and control her type 2 diabetes, an epidemic in America, with fifty-four million people having "pre-diabetes" and an additional twenty-one million suffering from the disease itself. According to the Centers for Disease Control and Prevention, type 2 diabetes is linked to obesity and physical inactivity, accounts for 90–95 percent of diabetes cases, and is now diagnosed among children and teens.[2]

Bennett knew she must tackle her disease. But something larger gnawed at her: her relationship with her daughter, who had been growing more distant every year—and who had recently told Bennett that she never wanted children, because of the state of the world. Bennett herself did not think she would live long enough to see a grandchild, anyway.

Bennett's personal sustainability practice (PSP) became the mechanism to tackle the broader health and relationship issues in her life. After many futile diets, her PSP paid off: she lost those seventy-five pounds, started getting control over her diabetes, and went off her medication—and most important, her daughter found her mother's efforts worth talking about.

The proof lies in the results. According to Walmart's first ever sustainability report, in the first seven months of sharing the Personal Sustainability Project with over a million Walmart associates, almost 45 percent of them voluntarily adopted and maintained a PSP.[3] Specifically, 19,924 Walmart associates quit or reduced smoking, and 375,824 associates shared the sustainability project with their friends, family, and community members outside Walmart. All told, they accomplished the following:

- Walked, biked, or swam a combined distance of more than 1.1 million miles

- Lost a combined weight of 184,315 pounds
- Recycled the following materials:
  - 675,538 pounds of aluminum
  - 282,476 pounds of glass
  - 6 million pounds of paper and cardboard
  - 3.2 million pounds of plastic

When leaders at the top unleash the power and creativity of their employees and then guide the organization as it goes through the TEN (transparency, engagement, and networking) cycle, they set the conditions to let everyone improve the company's strategy. Transparency empowers the trust that helps create engagement. The Walmart sustainability report that I quoted above was a sign from the company to its associates that their engagement mattered enough to be shared with the world. Engagement allows employees to do the STaR (society, technology, and natural resources) mapping that provides context for actions. These individual actions create ideas for innovation and provide a common framework for selecting which idea is important. Ideas for PSPs—from a person who teaches his or her family to recycle to somebody who adopts a local park to keep it clean—force employees to build a network outside the company. The network is the final part of the cycle, and employees will help build it.

This chapter explores ways that you, too—wherever you are within your organization and its network—can lead a strategy for sustainability. *It starts with you.*

Leaders Lead by Letting Go and Guiding the Process: The Case of Xerox

When Xerox CEO Anne Mulcahy took over the company in 2001, the vultures were already circling. Xerox was more than $17 billion in debt, and the Securities and Exchange Commission was investigating its accounting practices. The company had had an operating loss of $273 million the year before, it had lost $20 billion in stock market value between April 1999 and May 2000, and employee morale was at an all-time low. Xerox faced the very real possibility of bankruptcy.

Mulcahy's turnaround of Xerox is an object lesson in how the steps of a strategy for sustainability can be executed through steady leadership. The steps came naturally to her; as a longtime Xerox employee, she called on its traditions of innovation and community service to define her North Star in terms of changes in society, technology, and resources. By 2005, Xerox had gone from a $273 million annual loss to a $978 million gain. While many of the strategies she employed to get the company back on track simply reflected good management—for example, selling off nonessential businesses, reducing $1 billion in costs, spending her first ninety days visiting offices—she also accelerated business model changes that had begun in the early 1990s to move the world's greatest copier maker out of the business of selling copiers.

Today Xerox has almost sixty thousand employees in 160 countries. In 1959, Xerox cemented its reputation as one of the twentieth century's most innovative companies by releasing the Xerox 914, the first plain-paper copying machine, using a process called xerography. This dedication to R&D only intensified with the launch in 1970 of the famed Palo Alto Research Center (PARC). Over the next decade, Xerox PARC would become the birthplace of the technology behind the personal computer and the laser printer, neither of which, curiously, Xerox was ever able to exploit for its own market advantage.

Guiding the STaR Mapping

In 1993, Xerox hired Patty Calkins, a chemist at AT&T, to help it further integrate environmental design into its products and services. Xerox recognized that there were major changes coming in society, technology, and resources in 1993. The early 1990s represented the second great awakening of environmental thought in the United States, with the twentieth anniversary of Earth Day and the collision of the *Exxon Valdez* supertanker colliding to raise awareness to a level that hadn't been seen in the United States since the 1970s. Technology was threatening Xerox's competitive positioning. Foreign manufacturers were making inroads into the low-end product arena, a market that Xerox had at one point owned. In terms of resources, Xerox's corporate clients expected the company to collect the equipment once it was at the end of its life, and new regulations made disposal expensive.

Seeing this as the world ahead, Xerox set out a goal of "producing waste-free products in waste-free facilities to promote waste-free offices for our customers," a perfect example of a North Star goal.[4] The goal was something that inspired passion among employees. It was tied to a global human challenge, since electronic waste—*e-waste*—was beginning to mount up across the world. It connected to the core of the business, because Xerox began to market itself as in the business of document services, not copiers. Xerox had long been leasing its copiers, but increased the pace with the North Star goal of zero waste in mind. "We had these warehouses full of old copiers, and our repair teams were cannibalizing them for parts," said Calkins.[5] Covers and frames, for example, have a life longer than one machine. "And then we realized that if we design our products with remanufacturing in mind from the get-go, we could be moving quickly towards zero waste." Remanufacturing, the process of taking a used machine and renewing it so that it works as if it were brand new, became Xerox's obsession.

Unleashing the TEN Cycle

The first step for Xerox was to create a set of transparency initiatives so that the customer would know it was receiving a fully functioning product. "We developed technology called Signature Analysis that used test parameters to see what the useful life was in used parts and pieces. Our goal was to get to ninety percent reusability," said Calkins. When a product like a plastic soda bottle is recycled, it's frequently *downcycled*, that is, turned into another product (like a park bench) that uses a lower-quality plastic. When a product is remanufactured, parts are cleaned, repaired, and reused, which uses much less energy than what virgin products or downcycled materials require. Xerox helped develop an international standard (ISO 24700, "Quality and Performance of Office Equipments with Reused Parts") to guarantee quality and counter the stigma of "used" products among clients. The company also worked with cities and municipalities to change the language in their requests for proposals (RFPs) to accept certified remanufactured products.

Once Xerox engineers and designers were engaged in designing for remanufacturing, the breakthroughs began to accelerate. They produced a product with only 250 parts that originally had 2,000 parts. Xerox designed for commonality, so that components could be used in different models of equipment, reducing waste. It began using total life costing, so that even though the initial costs could be higher, Xerox would save money when the parts were used over and over. "The electromechanical parts needed to be built with more than one life in mind," said Calkins. Xerox even made new fasteners and bolts that sped up the disassembly of existing machines. In 2002, it recommitted to its energy goals by becoming part of the EPA's Climate Leaders program, committing to reducing its carbon use by 10 percent by 2012. Xerox formed ecoteams with senior executives, manufacturing operations, and its field service teams. One team focused on the toner business. Xerox's new emulsion aggregation toner uses much less energy to produce, but many of its customers still use old-fashioned powder toner, which needs to be ground in the production process. The toner team came up with the idea of adding an embrittling agent to the toner, which reduced energy use by 22 percent for grinding. Together, these steps outpaced their original goal, and Xerox reached a 10 percent reduction of carbon use by 2006.

But committing to the EPA Climate Leaders program wasn't the only way it used the network. The company became active in the industry associations working for remanufacturing and carbon regulation. It spent time educating customers on why they should care about building a sustainable business and how Xerox could save them money in the process. Xerox is the largest branded seller of cut sheet paper for copiers, so it joined with The Nature Conservancy to press its suppliers to certify that their paper came from sustainably harvested trees, and Xerox found new ideas for supply-chain improvements in the process.

Xerox estimates saving several hundreds of millions of dollars through its copier remanufacturing program. Nearly all Xerox-designed products are developed with remanufacturing and reuse in mind.

"In two thousand, we were worried about our survival," said Calkins. "But I was never worried about the fate of the work I was doing." She paused. "In that time of complexity, sustainability was a tool that helped us prioritize, and those longer-term priorities worked." Calkins sees companies that view sustainability as just compliance with laws and social stigmas as missing the point. "Companies that don't get it tend to fall back on just seeking to comply with what the outside world demands. That's actually more costly to the company. If you design something right from the front, it's going to cost you less than if you have to fix it when it breaks."

Leaders Put Business and Customer Values Before Popular Convention: The Case of Method

Method, a San Francisco-based household products company, may be the most successful consumer products company formed with a cra-dle-to-cradle approach to its products. The cradle-to-cradle process ensures that every ingredient is nontoxic and energy efficient throughout the process of production, use, and disposal. A simple way to look at it is that method considers the past, present, and future implications of every product it makes. Did the product come from a sustainable source (past)? Is it nontoxic (present)? Can it be reused or recycled (future)?

Founded in 2001 by Adam Lowry and Eric Ryan, method has quickly grown to $100 million in sales through wide distribution with retailers like Target and Lowe's. Its line of products extends from hand soaps to laundry detergents to cleaning sprays. All its products are recyclable, and a large portion is made with recycled content.

Despite all the time spent focusing on the sustainable aspects of its products, method does not describe itself solely as a "green" brand. "Green is one aspect of method," said Lowry. "It's not a marketing position."[6] Unlike other brands in household products that have different brand names in different categories, everything in method's product base has the method name. "Our brand is about a premium experience at home," said Lowry.

"There is tremendous pressure on environmentally conscious businesses to make green their primary message," he added. "But you need to be relevant to a wide audience, and leading with a single green message may exclude new consumers."

The method brand exemplifies one that could focus primarily on green but doesn't. A brand needs to have unique qualities, and green will not be a unique quality for long. Eventually, all products, because of competitive pressures, commodity costs, or regulation, will be nontoxic, energy-efficient, and sustainably packaged, at which point calling a product green won't do much. To truly be sustainable, a product needs more than just the environmental aspects of quality. "All that most of the green advertising is doing right now is signaling to consumers that your product is a member of the green category," said Lowry. For him, green is integral to the brand, not a way of marketing it.

Inside the walls of the method headquarters near San Francisco's Chinatown, a visitor can easily see why method describes itself as deep green on the inside. Lowry's job title is chief greenskeeper, and his role is to form and maintain a set of specific and unwavering principles that govern the functioning of the company.

One of method's principles is the precautionary principle that no product should be used unless it is proved to be safe. Lowry maintains a list of "dirty" chemicals that method won't use in any of its products, such as bleach, ammonia, and phthalates. Because method has yet to find an antimicrobial agent that is nonhazardous by its standards, the company doesn't currently sell any antimicrobial products like antibacterial hand wash.

It has a clean list, too, which constitutes the raw ingredients that method's product formulators, called green chefs, choose from. The company forms small teams to work on sustainable innovations and takes great care in choosing ingredients that are safe for people and the environment. It also makes sure that everyone at the company gets a chance to visit the San Francisco municipal waste facility to see where household products end up. This is also a way it ensures a high level of engagement among its staff.

There are five core values that method uses to guide the way it works:

1. Collaboration

2. Innovation

3. Care

4. What would MacGyver do?

5. Keep method weird

Including MacGyver, a reference to a 1980s television show whose title character is known for finding his way out of harrowing situations with a pocketknife and a few random objects, gives a good sense of the type of lean and crafty culture that method has created.

One of the more interesting things I find about method is how it deals with trade-offs. As "chief greenskeeper," Lowry is responsible for setting top-down policy through the principles and then providing coaching and technical support so that the staff can put the policies into action. But for a company so focused on saving resources, an ongoing challenge is to find design solutions that don't make trade-offs between design, efficacy, and environmental safety. The company's practices allow it to find unique solutions instead of trade-offs. One example is a bathroom scrub that method launched in 2008. The product is designed to hold a sponge, promoting the bottle's functionality beyond onetime use.

It would be possible for method to reduce the amount of plastic in some of its bottles by 5 percent, and if it did so, method would rank higher in a simple comparison of the minimum amount of materials used to package a product. But method believes that the design of the bottle is important to its brand and to its consumer, and occasionally, it takes 5 percent more plastic to make a beautiful bottle. So how does the company deal with this?

First, it accepts that "sustainable" isn't the only priority of its design ethos—aesthetics play an important role. Second, method makes sure that as much of the plastic that it does use is recycled and recyclable. Which leads to another hard choice.

In green consumer circles, dyes are considered evil, even though most products have dyes. At method, the company looks at the dyes and the product as a whole—the dyes on the bottle and the dyes in the liquid. It believes that if you run the life-cycle analysis on the dyes, it's much better to put the dyes in the liquid than on the bottle. Take, for example, method's all-purpose cleaner. It's put in a clear container made of 100 percent recycled polyethylene terephthalate (PET). The liquid inside that clear bottle is colored with 0.007 percent of a purple dye, which means there are micrograms of a dye in a whole bottle. "The dye is synthetic," said Lowry. "But it's completely degradable and nontoxic. It's a good dye."

A white PET bottle, on the other hand, may never get recycled. When white PET gets sorted in municipal recycling programs, the operators frequently think it's high-density polyethylene (HDPE), the stuff they make laundry bottles out of, and send it to the HDPE reprocessor. When it gets there, it gets punted out as an impurity and sent to a landfill. That white bottle uses a thousand times as much dye as method uses. "If you're going to want to tint a PET bottle white— you'll use a thousand times as much dye to dye the bottle—and you're going to make it less recyclable," Lowry said. "We want a plastic bottle that *will* be recycled—not just capable of being recycled."

To see how you stand in leadership toward sustainability, take this litmus test: What's your own version of method's clear-bottle-versus-dye trade-off? Can you name one trade-off you've accepted or rejected (in your life or work) in the last month? Method used training and research to make its choice. What tools did you use?

Leaders Have Generations of Customers in Mind: The Case of Seventh Generation

People have a strong and intimate connection to the household products they use. Perhaps that's why I'm so fascinated by how companies like P&G, Clorox, and method have approached the new wave of consumer interest in sustainable products. Unlike these relative newcomers to sustainability, the company Seventh Generation has been producing sustainable products long before doing so became trendy.

Five Native American tribes designed a constitution and formed the Iroquois Confederacy before Europeans arrived on their lands. Their territory stretched from what is today the Northeastern United States to Southern Canada.[7] Although many accounts focus on the Iroquois for their elaborate peace-making rituals, these people were also a warring tribe, known for fighting vicious "beaver wars" with the Mahican and Huron tribes to protect their beaver pelt monopoly with the Europeans.

Vermont-based Seventh Generation derives its name from the "great law" of the Iroquois Confederacy: "In our every deliberation, we must consider the impact of our decisions on the next

seven generations." Founded by Jeffrey Hollender, Seventh Generation's "Chief Inspired Protagonist" in 1988, Seventh Generation is
widely respected as one of the leading producers of sustainable
household products. And for more than a decade before new
entrants into the field began to innovate, Seventh Generation was
building a loyal following among consumers who were looking to
make a difference through the products they buy. When Hollender
founded the company, the concept of helping consumers use sustainability to help business improve the world was still new to the
United States. Business was about war making, and sustainability
was about peace making. The law of the Iroquois was a fitting
name, for it represented both the swords and the plowshares.

The company uses a set of global imperatives—goals that are
designed to be long term—to connect the operations of the business with the aspiration expressed in its name. The fundamental
question these imperatives answer is, What is Seventh Generation
uniquely able to do that the world most needs?

This question is a good litmus test for all business leaders. Can
you define what your company is uniquely able to do that the world
most needs?

Seventh Generation's global imperatives include the following:

- As a business, we are committed to being educators and to
  encourage those we educate to create with us a world of
  equity and justice, health and well-being.

- We believe that our business and all businesses should engage
  in the personal development of everyone who works for them.

- We are committed to approaching everything we do from a
  systems perspective, a perspective that allows us to see the
  larger whole, not a fragmented, compartmentalized world,
  not just what we want to see, our own point of view, our own
  reality, but a world that is endlessly interconnected, in which
  everything we do affects everything else.

- We must ensure that globally, natural resources are used and
  renewed at a rate that is always below their rate of depletion.

Hollender describes the goals as "scary, inspiring, hopeful, impossible, and awesome all at the same time" and credits them with changing how Seventh Generation does business.[8] Core to the ethos of Seventh Generation is that it believes that it can change society and how business works by succeeding in its own business. Forty years of organizational development research correlates this simple belief to high-performance employees and permanently infatuated customers.

Hollender is not your typical executive. He talks about a plan to transfer his company to employees over time. He gives away his corporate "secrets" by actively blogging. He even sent me large portions of a manuscript he was writing as I was interviewing him for this book. He refused to sell his products to Walmart before the retailer began its sustainability initiative, a decision that might have cost him millions of dollars. His rationale? He didn't want to be part of an institution that wasn't actively working to improve its social and environmental performance. He then spent many long hours in Bentonville, Arkansas, sharing his experience openly with Walmart leadership.

As a pioneer in his category and generally disposed to being generous with help, he has reacted in a very interesting way as nearly every major consumer packaged-goods company starts to enter the space. For the most part, Hollender is thrilled and points to the other companies as proof that his dream that business can change the world is coming true. He worries, though, about greenwashing and the effect this will have in making consumers skeptical about every product, including his. "A company that proclaims its commitment to social and environmental responsibility in a clumsy or inauthentic way quickly breeds cynicism and distrust—and invites the inevitable backlash," he said.

Sustainability needs to be core to the DNA of an organization. Hollender has seen many of his fellow entrepreneurs sell their companies to larger conglomerates. "Massive buyouts, minimal buy-in," is how he described the phenomenon. "Big-brand buyouts of natural products businesses . . . often act as a fig leaf for large corporations hoping to appropriate the virtues of the ethical company so as to rehabilitate their image." He remains hopeful. He is enjoying driving his business from the fringe to the center.

Here is another litmus test of sustainability: If your company's sales declined by 20 percent this year, would you still put focus on your strategy for sustainability? Can you define how your strategy for sustainability drives the core of your business?

Leaders Focus on Progress, Not Perfection: The Case of the Light Bulb

Attending a compact fluorescent light (CFL) summit in Las Vegas was strange. Las Vegas, a city painted onto a barren desert, dripping with wasted energy and water features, is more like a modern-day Sodom and Gomorrah than the place you'd expect to have an efficiency conference. It was like holding an optimism summit in London. Or a miniaturization conference in Texas. Or an alternative-energy conference in Saudi Arabia. The CFL summit in Las Vegas in 2006 had representatives from every major manufacturer, major retailers, lighting fixture makers, and nonprofits. There were so many of us, we filled a ballroom. Each of our tables had a centerpiece with CFLs that appeared to be growing out of plants.

A CFL can save hundreds or even thousands of dollars of electricity over its lifetime; the group together was committing to sell 200 million more of the light bulbs in the coming year: a clear win for the consumer and for the environment. But the meeting was rife with controversy.

Compact fluorescent light bulbs are not like the typical incandescent light bulbs that most people with electricity grew up with. The fluorescent bulbs have serious electronics and a small amount of mercury inside the base of the bulb. If the mercury is mishandled, it can be hazardous. The purpose of the conference was to get a nationwide marketing campaign to promote the bulbs, but we spent most of the time debating two issues. First, were the light bulbs good enough? The light bulb experts saw light-emitting diode (LED) technology coming quickly around the bend and thought that an interim step to CFLs was unwise. Another group was concerned about the mercury and the challenge that it caused. Fervent arguments ensued, with lots of strong opinions and wildly expressive hand gesticulations. Both of the concerns were valid issues, but they obscured the big picture. In the move toward sustainability, you have to accept small innovations that will lead to larger ones. Don't let your progress be stalled by your pursuit of perfection.

I was taught by legendary conservationist Ed Wayburn that to be a good leader, you needed to believe that incrementalism was not a crime. In the world of environmental activists, there are frequently debates about whether you're going far enough or whether you're a "compromiser." For Wayburn, compromise was never a problem, as along as forward motion continued. When we at the Sierra Club launched a public campaign to protect the entire Northern Rockies ecosystem, we were offered small sections of land that were far less than what we were asking for. We knew that large tracts of land had to be protected if the health of the ecosystem were to be maintained. We also knew that there was a risk that once we settled for a lesser amount of land, it would be harder to explain why the campaign would need to continue. Some activists criticized us for taking these half steps. But Wayburn had a rule. So long as we weren't taking a step backward by giving up a piece of land for improper development, we'd always take the deal. Success breeds success, innovation leads to innovation, and muscles need to work to grow.

Strong sustainability leaders need to champion incremental change as well as game-changing innovations. Once people accept that the products they've used their whole lives need to change, they'll be more willing to make changes more frequently. For corporations on top of the heap, this process will mean that they need to innovate constantly. Upstart competitors will have the opportunity to break into new categories, since all of this rapid change will tend to destabilize the relationships with their existing products.

Back in Las Vegas, the advocates for spreading the CFL technology eventually won the day at the summit, and over 200 million of those bulbs were sold in the following year in the United States. More important, the bulbs taught the consumer an important lesson about paying more for something that will last longer and save money.

One key reason to constantly be prepared to innovate is that the science of sustainability and technology are moving faster than we could predict. Liquid crystal display (LCD) flat-screen televisions and monitors have been heralded as a great step forward for both energy efficiency and waste concerns, compared with traditional cathode-ray tube (CRT) monitors. But a recent scientific study has shown that a chemical used in the cleaning and manufacture of LCD screens for everything from cell phones to laptops is seventeen thousand times more harmful than CO_2, which is the most pervasive greenhouse gas. Nitrogen trifluoride, or NF_3, lasts 550 years in the atmosphere and is a rapidly growing contributor to climate change.[9] The NF_3 emissions on the planet in 2008 equal the total greenhouse gas emissions of Austria. Ironically, NF_3 came into widespread use as manufacturers tried to find a substitute for perfluorocarbons, another group of greenhouse gases, but they hoped that the NF_3 would be more carefully contained in the production process.

I asked Tod Arbogast from Dell how his company deals with this shifting landscape and shifting expectations. "It's not that surprising," he said. "We moved from CRTs to LCDs, and that was a good thing." He paused. "Now I'm hearing the momentum to move from LCDs to the highly energy-efficient OLED technology." OLED refers to the new organic light-emitting diode technology that will take the place of LCDs. Companies that are prepared to change can make more changes when the time is right. The new sustainability leader will be prepared to celebrate a victory and move on to the next milestone, sometimes contemporaneously.

The challenge with all this "progress" is that it shouldn't be an excuse for churning through products and materials that are perfectly fine. In the electronics realm, they call this *planned obsolescence*, the process of making a product nonfunctional after a certain amount of time. Manufacturers call this *shortening the replacement cycle* and use planned obsolescence to reduce the time between repeat purchases of their products. Applying the lens of sustainability, the best strategy is to have hardware that can be upgraded when technology improves. The moment when a product no longer functions is a chance for a user to change brands, and reducing the possibility by allowing a user to upgrade existing hardware can mean retaining a customer.

When Apple launched the iPod, users were unable to change the battery themselves or update the firmware (the software built into the device). On the other hand, when Microsoft released the Zune, the product had upgradable firmware, so that you didn't need to throw out the device when the technology became out-of-date. Taking this out even further, Jim Thomas, the vice president for corporate social responsibility at JCPenney, once told me his dream of having clothing that is "updated" with a new season's designs electronically in the same way an image on a computer screen changes.[10] In this mode, clothiers would be selling the electronic designs while the basic clothes would last for many years. While this might be far off, the idea of having a laptop whose hard drive and central processing unit would be upgraded while the chassis remained unchanged is here today.

In the meantime, there are small changes that companies and countries are already making. All cell phones in South Korea use the same power adapter. When you buy a cell phone, it doesn't come with an adapter, because you can use the one that you had for your last cell phone. If you forget your adapter, you can borrow one from a friend, since they're all the same. Do you have a drawer full of obsolete power adapters? I do. What if consumers worldwide were delighted by competing companies' coming together to create a common plug that would reduce waste and simplify their lives? This would be one step toward less waste in cell phones, which on average are discarded every eighteen months. Eventually, cell phones will have much longer lives and will be built to be upgraded rather than destroyed. But in the meantime, a step toward standardized plugs is a good first step—training wheels to a larger leap forward. When you're starting a new business, sometimes you can take the training wheels off and go all the way to start.

Here's a sustainability pop quiz: What's one small thing you will do differently today?

Act Now: Move from Green to Blue

Reducing carbon dioxide was one part of the Xerox turnaround strategy, but the effort went far beyond a typical green program, and so must you if you hope to lead a sustainable business. As twenty-first-century companies structure themselves for the turbulent times ahead, they need to break down the old categories of philanthropy, compliance, and performance to actually create a strategy for sustainability. To merely comply is not to lead. The world needs a new type of leader who can think past the old rhetoric to find business opportunity in solving the social challenges of our time. The place to start is by having conversations with your colleagues about sustainability.[11]

Words are important, and we need to evolve our lexicon if we're going to succeed in moving sustainability out of the realm of philanthropy and compliance and into the realm of opportunity and long-term growth (table 7-1).[12] That's why it's time to move beyond green as the color and gestalt of the sustainability movement. After all, only a small part of the world is green; it's mostly blue.

The color blue is already popping up around the world as the symbol of the sustainability movement, from the mature green marketplaces in Nordic countries to island nations like Japan and New Zealand, to rapidly developing economies like China's that are fighting poverty as well as environmental threats. As I see it, blue integrates all four aspects of sustainability—social, economic, environmental, and cultural—and puts people at the center of the

TABLE 7-1

Move your leadership language from green to blue

Green Manifesto	Blue Manifesto
We have strong environmental values.	We have strong social, economic, environmental, and cultural values.
There are limits and constraints.	There are possibilities and opportunities.
We must make food organic.	We can all eat sustainably.
We need government action.	We need government, market, and community collaboration.
It is our obligation, our responsibility.	It is our passion, our aspiration.
We have hope for the planet.	We have faith in people.
We must stop the madness.	I will change my behavior and invite you to join me.
The world may not survive for our children.	We can act now and do something for today and for the future.

conversation. As an advocate, you care as much about the effect of a high utility bill on a family struggling to pay for health care, or about the crisis in the planet's atmosphere, as you care about the price you're paying for fuel. All of these crises need solving.

But even the right words and the right framework won't create leaders, and understanding the pacing for sustainability is critical. Evolutionary biologists use the concept of punctuated equilibrium to describe the phenomenon that many organisms experience little change until rapid events of evolution occur. Evolutionary steps seem to go slow for a very long time, and then, in a burst of motion, everything skips forward. Punctuated equilibrium (or "punk-eek," as the biologists call it) is a good metaphor for how you'll move forward with sustainability.

Sometimes, changes will come rapidly because of events that are outside our control. Consider how the nuclear industry began to be regulated after the meltdown of the Chernobyl reactor. Consider how the business of oil transportation changed after the *Exxon Valdez* ship ran aground in Prince William Sound. Consider the speed at which the Montreal Protocol regulated chlorofluorocarbons (CFCs) after the stark image of the ozone hole was shown to the world. Consider how the Seveso disaster, in which a cloud of

TCDD, a highly toxic form of dioxin, was accidentally released over eleven communities in Italy in 1976, birthed Europe's muscular approach to toxics. But while spectacular and devastating events will no doubt occur, it's not good strategy to simply wait for bad news before a person or a company changes.

That's why I believe in both going for game changers *and* incremental steps that move toward a sustainable world. In a business context, it's about making a business use one innovation to drive the next innovation. It's about using successive small steps to get where you want to go. Once you experience self-efficacy—the belief that your actions can make a difference—you tend to take more steps forward. One thing leads to another. Even something as simple as changing to compact fluorescent light bulbs is a good example of a step that's an invitation to more change.

Conclusion

L EO TOLSTOY began his novel *Anna Karenina* with the
sentence "Happy families are all alike; every unhappy
family is unhappy in its own way." Sustainability leaders are largely
alike in their drive forward; every laggard has his own excuse for
doing nothing. Most people, when trying to transform their company, find a raft of reasons why their company is uniquely unquali-
fied to change now. They're too small, or too big. They're too much
of a manufacturer or too much of a service business. They're in the
middle of a succession process or they haven't yet begun one.
They're growing wildly or shrinking precipitously. They're too new
or too old. As far as I'm concerned, as long as the instigators of the
effort are committed, there is no right time and no wrong time, up
economy or down economy, so you might as well start now.

Let's not forget why we're talking about sustainability in the
first place. When we analyze the world from a STaR perspective, the
reasons for changing from current business strategy for short-term

profitability to a strategy for sustainability are clear. The global economy, our environment, and political institutions are undergoing rapid structural change.

The global population will soon reach nine billion people, forcing major demographic shifts because the most rapidly growing populations will be in emerging markets like Brazil, Russia, India, and China. The social, political, and environmental risks that companies face in working in these countries are growing in kind. Nineteen cities will have over twenty million people in the twenty-first century.[1] Everything is connected in these major cities, where a shock to one system, from a recession to a disease outbreak, will rapidly reverberate around the world through global commerce and air travel. Governments are too local to solve these cross-border issues, leaving corporations uniquely liable and qualified to protect their operating environment. If corporations don't act, then nongovernmental actors from community organizations to investor groups will begin to publicize and punish slackers for lax safety and environmental performance, which will be amplified by new communications technology.

Meanwhile, the developing world still seeks basic necessities like basic health care, with nearly one million people dying each year from preventable and treatable malaria.[2] Over 820 million people on the planet will go to sleep hungry tonight. The developed world faces its own problems.

A much larger number of people, roughly 1.6 billion, are suffering from the effects of having too much to eat and being overweight.[3] Consider that fact for a moment. Twice as many people on the planet are dealing with the problems of too much food as are dealing with the problems of too little. This is the modern paradox. We live in a time of paucity and plenty. Of the costs in the U.S. health-care system, 80 percent come from five major diseases— heart disease, diabetes, asthma, cancer, obesity—all of which can be moderated or prevented through behavior changes, and yet Americans refuse to change. America is the wealthiest nation in history, yet Americans tell pollsters that things are getting worse.

In both the developing world and the developed world, this state of affairs is not sustainable.

Decades ago, Adlai Stevenson, the U.S. Ambassador to the United Nations, said:

> *We travel together, passengers on a little spaceship, dependent on its vulnerable reserves of air and soil; all committed, for our safety, to its security and peace; preserved from annihilation only by the care, the work and the love we give our fragile craft. We cannot maintain it half fortunate, half miserable, half confident, half despairing, half slave—to the ancient enemies of man—half free in a liberation of resources undreamed of until this day. No craft, no crew can travel safely with such vast contradictions. On their resolution depends the survival of us all.*[4]

While the problems Stevenson references—war, poverty, environmental degradation, and disrespected or unprotected human rights—are as acute today as they were in the last century, there is no better opportunity than now for businesses to play a critical role in resolving these challenges, *while building their businesses.* Ultimately, this is what separates a strategy for sustainability from the philanthropic orientation of corporate social responsibility projects.

Indeed, many of the social and environmental trends I've laid out above are sad, tragic, even unjust, but sustainability is not about throwing your business down the drain and embracing your inner do-gooder. That's one reason to look past the green aspects of sustainability to include the broader call for social, economic, and cultural sustainability as tools to build your business. While green businesses, green jobs, and emerging green economies will be a central part of the new world we're creating together, green alone is not a broad enough platform to sustain most businesses for the long haul.

The rationale behind building a sustainable business that takes into account these broader social issues is straightforward. Businesses that are capable of dealing with the complex challenges of a changing world will be better able to build a business prepared to respond and lead. And companies large and small are already beginning to lead.

When one of the world's largest snack-food makers, Frito-Lay, recognized that society's changing expectations meant it had to make healthier snacks using more wholesome manufacturing processes, it launched new brands like SunChips, a whole-grain snack. Created in 1991, SunChips has experienced phenomenal growth of nearly 20 percent a year, making it one of the fastest-growing snack products in the PepsiCo organization. The ingredients in it are simple, whole corn, sunflower oil, whole wheat, rice flour, whole oat flour, sugar, and salt. Not only are these snacks more nutritious, they are beginning to be made with equipment powered by solar energy. SunChips powered by the sun—a brilliant alignment of product, brand, and sustainability. The payoff? Frito-Lay found itself with one of its fastest-growing new brands in a decade.

Gannon Jones is a vice president of marketing for Frito-Lay North America, with over $11 billion in annual sales. He oversees growth brands, and has helped implement the philosophy of nanopractices—small things people do each day that make sustainability real—as a core piece of their brand strategy. He says, "Within all of us there exists a timeless tension between the desire to do better and our unwillingness to change."[5] Frito-Lay is helping its consumers navigate toward improving their lives.

At the beginning of the decade, Frito-Lay had noticed an emerging intersection among its consumers between concern for health and concern for the planet—a clear opportunity to accelerate the company's corporate focus on growing its business in healthier snacks while emphasizing those health credentials. The linkage to sustainability was natural.

In 2008, we worked with Frito-Lay as it was figuring out how to communicate the launch of a solar array that would provide some of the power to make SunChips in its Modesto, California, plant. It chose not to focus on a purely green message strategy, and instead has placed its green efforts into the more comprehensive "small steps" framework.

"Most consumers still are looking for a tangible, functional benefit in making a purchase decision, one that can be complemented by a 'green' benefit," said Jones. SunChips found that the combined benefit of health and sustainability was more motivating than either of them separately. Sustainability enabled Frito-Lay to demonstrate the integrity and authenticity of the brand and reinforce the healthier aspects of the chips.

"Our consumers still buy SunChips primarily because it is a healthier choice . . . the fact that they are made with the help of solar energy is an added bonus." Jones notes two similar cases. He says that people buy compact fluorescent light bulbs mostly because they save money, and they buy the Toyota Prius because it get better gas mileage.

How did Frito-Lay communicate about its efforts without being tagged a greenwasher? According to Jones, the first reason is that sustainability is core to their business strategy. "We believe that in order to be successful and credible, you must embrace sustainability as a core business strategy . . . not a promotional tactic." For SunChips, this meant committing to making strides across all aspects of its business model.

While Frito-Lay has had a strong resource-conservation program since 1999, the efforts behind SunChips started in 2007 with purchasing renewable energy credits to offset its electricity needs (as part of an overall PepsiCo purchase). The company then expanded its efforts to improving its manufacturing practices by powering its Modesto plant with solar power, working on reducing the environmental impact of its packaging, and getting involved with reputable sustainability initiatives.

The second key to its success was its humility in emphasizing its small steps. No grandstanding. "We have continually ensured that we are talking about what we are doing or have already done . . . not what we may or may not do at some point in the distant future." Those criticized for "greenwashing" are often guilty of violating one or both of these principles.

For SunChips, sustainability has been integral to the brand's continued success. Jones points out that sustainability "has allowed us to differentiate ourselves from competitors. It has provided opportunities to integrate and work closely with our key retailer partners who share our sustainability vision. It has given us signifi-cant media coverage for our efforts, which have helped raise overall awareness of the brand. And our consumers have enthusiastically embraced our efforts."

But all of this is just the entrance point to its core proposition: that SunChips is a small step that people can take to improve their lives. "Our consumers have discovered a simple truth . . . that by breaking things down into small manageable pieces, they are more likely to reach their goals," says Jones. Jones acknowledges that if SunChips tasted like cardboard it wouldn't work. For the consumer, choosing a "heart-healthy" chip is an attempt to live bet-ter, and probably only one small step among a host of others. "Our approach has been to talk to them about our steps towards a 'healthier planet' . . . and encourage them to take their own," he says.

Small steps matter. And that's one reason I've encouraged you in this book to promote sustainable nanopractices. Instead of focus-ing solely on the game-changing win, the small steps prepare your organization for the turbulence facing our world.

Fortunately, the business world is ripe for a change. Companies that appeared to be built to last have found themselves stranded on the rocks of societal change, while upstarts that have sustainabil-ity programmed into their DNA have continued to thrive. In fact, the companies tracked by the Goldman Sachs Sustain framework, which examines management effectiveness by looking at how they respond to environmental, social, and governance issues, have out-performed market indices since the framework's creation. In Gold-man Sachs's estimation, this proves that companies that can manage their risks and opportunities can manage their companies for the long haul.[6]

I've avoided focusing on the brand value and goodwill that can be built by creating a strategy for sustainability. Why? Because brand value is a byproduct of an integrated corporate strategy, not the main focus of that strategy. Kevin Roberts, global CEO of Saatchi & Saatchi, says bluntly, "Brands today are dead. They have become commodified, performance based, functionally driven and sold through old school selling by yelling techniques."[7] The result, he says, is that, "Consumers are up in arms. Power has switched from brands to consumers and the Information Age has liberated all of us so that no brand can hide now behind its packaging or its positioning." According to Roberts, sustainability is a strategy for a brand to reconnect with the consumer by transparently sharing the brand's problems and solutions. That's quite a change from the old model of selling soap because it smells fresh and cleans deeply.

In this book we've examined transparency in a number of ways. Procter & Gamble used a lifecycle analysis, a tool for value-chain transparency, to see that its greatest impact was in the hot water its customers were using to wash clothes, and used that insight to create Tide Coldwater. Nike used transparency to help its designers understand how they could use fewer materials to produce high performance shoes. Clorox printed the ingredients on the packaging on its Greenworks line of cleaners to demonstrate authenticity to their customers. All of these uses together equal the transparent authenticity that Roberts is describing.

The key is that these products perform better because they were built with a strategy for sustainability in mind. There is no end to the possible solutions we can create. According to the Texas Transportation Institute, "Traffic congestion continues to worsen in American cities of all sizes, creating a $78 billion annual drain on the U.S. economy in the form of 4.2 billion lost hours and 2.9 billion gallons of wasted fuel—that's 105 million weeks of vacation and 58 fully loaded supertankers."[8] Through enhancing public transportation and using "smart" traffic signal software systems, the United

States could save billons of dollars in fuel and much more in lost productivity by American workers who are sick of commuting. Similarly, the electric grid in the United States wastes billions of dollars of energy a year by leaking energy, which could be improved by smart-grid technology. There are thousands of products and systems that can be improved by squeezing out waste and taking a long-term view that has been sorely missed in the last two decades.

Ask anyone who went through the global stock market crash of 2008 whether they would have chosen a strategy for sustainability instead of a strategy for short-term profit and they would probably choose the former. After all, the most basic rule of sustainability is to never irreparably destroy your capital. People who tried to squeeze an extra 3 or 4 percent return out of their portfolio but lost 40 percent of their net worth wondered if the extra stretch was worth it. Employees who were laid off would rather have worked for a company that had been prepared for a contraction. People who bought a house they could not afford knew they were better off waiting until they could afford it.

After the crash, people tried to protect what they had, hoping that external events wouldn't overtake their old strategy, which they had thought to be "balanced." But if your portfolio is now worth 60 percent of what it was before, it's not exactly sustaining itself. Sustainability means meeting your needs now while not compromising your ability to meet your future needs. Despite the marble or brass on the facade, many a failed bank didn't have sustainability in its strategy. That's why I feel so passionately that CEOs and the board, employees and managers, business students and professors, must heed the lessons of sustainability that the companies inside this book can offer. It is a once-in-a-lifetime opportunity to build companies that are prepared for a future and its inevitable shocks. If you must rightsize your staffing today to respond to a crisis, then you can plan your comeback so that you need not experience such wild swings in performance again. Your task is to build the capabilities of sustainability: transparency, engagement and networks, deep into your organization. No matter how small or big, it's always the right time to begin.

In the wake of the global stock market crash, commentators searched for an analog from history to explain what was happening. But the 24/7 news channels and always-on Internet sites only increased the general apprehension of the moment. Panics occur when people get conflicting information from a barrage of authorities. You don't know where to run and what to do.

Obviously, solving problems once they've occurred is a lot more costly than preventing them altogether. Analysts who looked to the U.S. stock market crash in 1933 or the Japanese economic meltdown in the 1980s were searching for an answer to the questions, "When the bubble bursts, how do we minimize the pain?" But what if instead we asked the question, "How do we build a bubble-proof company?"

For the task of creating companies that are truly sustainable, we have a much greater pool of information than the few market events of the twentieth century: we have millions of years of natural history. We have catastrophic failures, like the Galveston flood of 1900, the 1931 Yellow and Yangtze river floods that killed four million people, the European heat waves of 2003, the 2004 Tsunami off the west coast of Sumatra, Indonesia, and the Australian wildfires of 2009.[9] Nature is harsher than the market; if you're not sustainable you die. No second chances and no bailouts, just death and maybe extinction for your entire species.

Every crisis is an opportunity. This crisis is our chance—your chance—to rebuild it right. Build a strategy for sustainability into the core of your company and your life.

Douglas Adams, author of the *Hitchhiker's Guide to the Galaxy* series, once said, "If you try and take a cat apart to see how it works, the first thing you have on your hands is a non-working cat. Life is a level of complexity that almost lies outside our vision; it is so far beyond anything we have any means of understanding that we just think of it as a different class of object, a different class of matter; 'life,' something that had a mysterious essence about it . . ."[10]

When a situation seems too complicated to grasp, grasping it isn't always entirely necessary or even possible—so do what you can, when you can.

Act now.

Acknowledgments

Let me start by acknowledging that I'm responsible for everything wrong in this book, and the people I mention below are responsible for everything else. The ideas here have been forged collectively by the people of Saatchi & Saatchi S through the messy work of building and executing business strategies for some of the world's most influential companies.

I feel fortunate to have been given the time to write this book and the invitation to co-create the ideas inside by Kevin Roberts and Saatchi & Saatchi and Andy Murray of Saatchi & Saatchi X. Under the stewardship of Bill Cochrane and Milano Reyna, they have made Saatchi & Saatchi the guinea pig for everything in this book.

For those who knew David Brower, they'll see a lot of him in this book, and hardly a week goes by when I don't miss his advice and mentorship. Similarly, Paul Hawken's work to create the canvas of sustainable business has been deeply influential to me, and I feel lucky to have had his support and guidance over the years. I am patiently waiting for the Nobel committee to recognize his work. Andy Ruben, more than any other single person, drafted me into the work of corporate transformation and I wish he could have been the coauthor of this book. My outlook on the possibilities for progress changed radically once I began to spend weeks in Walmart stores and as I was invited into the homes of the associates who work at Walmart. This book is not the story of Walmart's transformation; but I can't wait for that book to be written.

Deeply frustrated at the progress of the environmental movement in 2003, I worked with Peter Teague of the Nathan Cummings Foundation and Michael Shellenberger and Ted Nordhaus, now of the Breakthrough Institute, and with Irene Hughes on the ideas that would lead to my speech "Is Environmentalism Dead?" Many of those ideas underpin the thinking in *Strategy for Sustainability*. I first met Vice President Al Gore when, as a senator considering a run for the presidency, he was on a fact-finding trip. I received a master class in the fundamentals of climate change and have had his encouragement over the years; I'm still amazed that he could make a PowerPoint slide show sexy. Both Amory and Hunter Lovins, each in their own way—Amory with his Yiddish songs and orangutans, Hunter with her Scotch and passion for teaching—have helped guide the content herein. Jib Ellison's work in supporting Walmart's transformation enabled my own; he is one of the finest consultants on the planet.

In writing this book I was fortunate to have a cast of characters to lend their help, as the world seemed to implode as I was writing. I am wildly happy with the support I've received from Harvard Business Press, notably the wisdom, grace, and advocacy of my editor Kirsten Sandberg. After this book, my agent, Dan Strone, owes me another harrowing sea kayak or whitewater trip, and I expect to collect. From Saatchi & Saatchi S, Noel Vietor, Ben Grant, and former SSC activist Elizabeth Hagan buoyed me with their endless enthusiasm and aid for this project as deadlines drew near. Melissa Price, one of the most talented writers I know, was kind enough to edit early drafts for me. My original partners at Act Now, David Steuer, Judah Schiller, and Lyn, have been the best mates one could hope for on this ride as our passionate, obscure work suddenly became mainstream.

There are dozens of stories in this book that came directly from my Facebook network. I set my status to the subject I was writing about and in turn received ideas and sources. Thank you.

I'm blessed with three kids under five years old, so it has taken a village of support to give me the time to travel around the world to do my research, in particular Jessica Tully, Tara Kurland, and Jordan Kurland. My parents, Mel and Gail, and my brother, Kevin, continue to inspire me. Finally, to my love Lyn. THANK YOU, THANK YOU, THANK YOU, I promise I'll put my computer away now. I love you.

Transparency: Transparency is a core principle of *Strategy for Sustainability*. I have indicated every company with which I have worked directly in the text of the book and tried to be as fair as possible in my descriptions.

Notes

Introduction

1. Jeff Williams, "Louisiana Coastal Wetlands: A Resource at Risk," U.S. Geological Survey, Marine and Coastal Geology Program fact sheet, 3 November 1993, http://marine.usgs.gov/fact-sheets/LAwetlands/lawetlands.html.

2. Stephen Ackroyd, Rosemary Batt, Paul Thompson, and Pauls S. Tolbert, *The Oxford Handbook of Work and Organization* (Oxford: Oxford University Press, 2006).

3. http://www.forbes.com/2007/01/30/wal-mart-comps-the-world-biz-cx_tvr_0131 walmart.html.

4. http://www.stwr.org/imf-world-bank-trade/reforming-international-trade.html.

5. Alisa Priddle Alisa and Robert Snell, "Plane Facts: GM Cutting Back Fleet, Automaker Downsizing to 3 Jets; Chrysler Owns None While Mulally, Family Use Ford Aircraft," *Detroit News,* 22 November 2008, www.detnews.com/apps/pbcs.dll/article?AID=/20081122/AUTO01/811220359/0/SPECIAL.

6. Office of the House Republican Leader, "Boehner Statement on Auto Bailout Proposal from House & Senate Democrats," press release, 13 November 2008, http://republicanleader.house.gov/News/DocumentSingle.aspx?DocumentID=105734.

7. Rocky Mountain Institute, RMI and MOVE, FAQ Web page, 2008, http://move.rmi.org/features/faqs.html#bestway.

8. Michael Levine, "Why Bankruptcy Is the Best Option for GM," *Wall Street Journal,* 17 November 2008, http://online.wsj.com/article/SB12268863 1448632421.html.

9. Stephen Cooney and Brent Yacobucci, "U.S. Automotive Industry: Policy Overview and Recent History," *Congressional Research Service Report for Congress,* Library of Congress, 25 April 2005, http://ncseonline.org/NLE/CRS reports/05apr/RL32883.pdf.

10. Office of the Speaker of the House, "Pelosi to Auto Industry: Show Us a Plan for Viability," press release, 20 November 2008, http://speaker.house.gov/newsroom/pressreleases?id=0893.

11. Brundtland Report, 4 August 1987.

12. Michael Pollan, "Our Decrepit Food Factories," *New York Times,* 16 December 2007, www.nytimes.com/2007/12/16/magazine/16wwln-lede-t.html? ref=health.

13. Michael Pollan, "Why Bother?" *New York Times,* 20 April 2008, www. nytimes.com/2008/04/20/magazine/20wwln-lede-t.html?_r=1& pagewanted=1&ref=magazine.

14. Daniel C. Esty and Andrew S. Winston, *Green to Gold: How Smart Companies Use Environmental Strategy to Innovate, Create Value, and Build Competitive Advantage* (New Haven, CT: Yale University Press, 2006).

15. Adam Werbach and Auden Schendler, interview by Sheilah Kast, "The Business of Green," *On Point with Tom Ashbrook,* NPR, 21 November 2007, www.onpointradio.org/shows/2007/11/the-business-of-green. In the interview, Schendler suggested that gas should cost ten dollars a gallon, and we discussed the implications.

16. Toyota is a significant client of Saatchi & Saatchi, which was intimately involved with the launch of the Prius.

17. Ford Motor Company, "Remarks by Alan Mulally, President and CEO, Ford Motor Company, at the 2008 Annual Meeting of Shareholders," press release, 8 May, 2008, www.ford.com/about-ford/news-announcements/press-releases/press-releases-detail/pr-remarks-by-alan-mulally-president-28206.

18. Ibid.

19. James C. Collins and Jerry I. Porras, *Built to Last: Successful Habits of Visionary Companies* (New York: HarperBusiness, 1994).

20. Henry Ford and Samuel Crowther, *My Life and Work* (Montana: Kessinger, 2003), 73.

21. Ford Motor Company, "Remarks by Alan Mulally."

22. Fara Warner, "How Ford Lost Focus," *Mother Jones,* November–December 2008, www.motherjones.com/news/feature/2008/11/losing-focus.html.

23. Christine Tierney, "Toyota Sees Record '07 Profit," *Detroit News,* 8 November 2007, www.detnews.com/apps/pbcs.dll/article?AID=/20071108/ AUTO01/711080360/1148.

24. Toyota Corporation, "A New Year's Greeting from Toyota President Katsuaki Watanabe," press release, 1 January 2008, www.theautochannel.com/ news/2007/12/31/074153.html.

25. J. Liker, "The 14 Principles of the Toyota Way: An Executive Summary of the Culture Behind TPS," www.si.umich.edu/ICOS/Liker01.pdf.

26. Toyota Corporation, "Plans for Realizing Sustainable Mobility," http://www.toyota.co.jp/en/ir/presentation/2008/pdf/081002presen_2.pdf.

27. Toyota Sustainability Report, http://www.toyota.co.jp/en/csr/report/08/ special/02.html.

28. Saatchi & Saatchi provides marketing services for Toyota, having helped launch the hybrid Prius.

29. Caterpillar Inc., "Caterpillar to Expand Remanufacturing Business with Acquisition of Certain Gremada Industries," Thomson Reuters Inc. press release, 16 June 2008, www.reuters.com/article/pressRelease/idUS133430+ 16-Jun-2008+PRN20080616.

30. "Anheuser-Busch to Pour 5 Billion Green Beers in 2009," *Environmental Leader,* 31 May 2008, www.environmentalleader.com/2008/07/30/anheuser-busch-to-pour-5-billion-green-beers-in-2009/.

31. International Air Transportation Association, "Industry Bids Farewell to Paper Ticket," press release, May 31, 2008, www.iata.org/pressroom/pr/2008-31-05-01.htm.

32. Research Recap, "Herman Miller: How Profits and Sustainability Parallel," *Seeking Alpha,* 4 August 2008, http://seekingalpha.com/article/88921-herman-miller-how-profits-and-sustainability-parallel.

Chapter One

1. If you are interested in learning more about California chaparral, I recommend the Web site of the California Chaparral Institute, www.california chaparral.org.

2. James Wallace, "Aerospace Notebook: Fuel-Saving Winglets Tried on Boeing 767," *Seattle Post Intelligencer,* 22 July 2008, http://seattlepi.nwsource. com/business/371786_air23.html.

3. In the field of biology, E. O. Wilson's works stand out as particularly important for this book. Similarly, the work of Janine Benyus and the Biomimicry Guild is critical. Steven Vogel's work in biomechanics has been deeply influential to me as well. I should note that I have had significant disagreements with both Wilson and members of the biomimicry field in years past over issues of how these researchers place environmental issues over human concerns.

4. Charles Darwin, *The Origin of Species by Means of Natural Selection, or the Preservation of Favoured Races in the Struggle for Life,* 6th ed. (London: John Murray, 1872).

5. Stephen Jay Gould, *Ever Since Darwin* (New York: Norton, 1977).

6. Michael Begon, Colin R. Townsend, and John L. Harper, *Ecology: From Individuals to Ecosystems,* 4th ed. (Oxford: Blackwell, 2005).

7. R. L. Kitchin, *Systems Ecology: an Introduction to Ecological Modeling* (St. Lucia, Australia: University of Queensland Press, 1983); Eugene Odum, Richard Brewer, and Gary W. Barrett, *Fundamentals of Ecology,* 5th ed. (Pacific Grove, CA: Brooks Cole, 2004); Aldo Leopold, *Round River: From the Journals of Aldo Leopold* (New York: Oxford University Press, 1953).

8. Janine Benyus, *Biomimicry: Innovation Inspired by Nature* (New York: William Morrow, 1997).

9. John Thompson, *The Geographic Mosaic of Coevolution* (Chicago: University of Chicago, 2005).

10. Paul Hawken, *The Ecology of Commerce: A Declaration of Sustainability* (New York: Harper Collins, 1993); Herman Daly and Joshua Farley, *Ecological Economics, Principles and Applications* (Washington, DC: Island Press, 2004).

11. Michael Braungart and William McDonough, *Cradle to Cradle: Remaking the Way We Make Things* (New York: North Point Press, 2002); Walter Stahel, *The Performance Economy* (Basingstoke, UK: Palgrave Macmillan, 2006).

12. Robert Costanza et al., "The Value of the World's Ecosystem Services and Natural Capital," *Nature,* 15 May 1987, 253–260.

13. Jim Hartzfeld, e-mail, 1 January 2009.

14. Chuck Tryon, phone conversation, 4 August 2008.

15. Lance Ulanoff, "Google's 20 Percent Time Drives Innovation," *PC Magazine,* 7 February 2009, http://www.pcmag.com/article2/0,2817,2340545,00.asp.

16. Gary Flake, "The Live Labs Manifesto," 22 June 2006, http://livelabs.com/blog/the-live-labs-manifesto/.

17. Sara Yirrell, "A Break in the Circuit," *CRN,* 13 November 2008, www.channelweb.co.uk/crn/comment/2230468/break-circuit-4344908.

18. In *Good to Great* (New York: HarperCollins, 2001), 7, Jim Collins examined eleven companies that had improved for fifteen years after a "transition" point when their management had materially changed. The two top-performing companies on the list were Circuit City (which had grown 18.5 times the market) and Fannie Mae (which had grown 7.56 times the market). Both of these would teeter on the verge of bankruptcy in 2008, examples of companies without a strategy for sustainability.

19. Ibid., 55.

20. Anita Hamilton, "Why Circuit City Busted, While Best Buy Boomed," *Time,* 11 November 2008, www.time.com/time/business/article/0,8599,1858079,00.html.

21. Paul Asquith, Michael B. Mikhail, and Andrea S. Au, "Information Content of Equity Analyst Reports," *Journal of Financial Economics* 75, no. 2 (February 2005): 245–282.

22. John R. Graham, Campbell R. Harvey, and Shiva Rajgopal, "Value Destruction in Financial Reporting Decisions," *Financial Analysts Journal* 62, no. 6 (November/December 2006): 27–39.

23. National Ethanol Vehicle Coalition, "Flexible Fuel Vehicles," 29 September 2006, www.biotenn.org/docs/pdf/05-18-07%20FFV%20List%202007.pdf.

Chapter Two

1. Boris Worm et al., "Impacts of Biodiversity Loss on Ocean Ecosystem Services," *Science,* 3 November 2006: 787–790.

2. Ibid. For a general summary of Worm et al.'s work, see Cornelia Dean, "Study Sees 'Global Collapse' of Fish Species," *New York Times,* 3 November 2006, www.nd.edu/~jwarlick/documents/UnsustainableFishing.pdf.

3. Christopher L. Delgado et al., *Fish to 2020: Supply and Demand in Changing Global Markets,* part 3 (Washington, DC: International Food Policy Research Center, 2003), www.ifpri.org/pubs/books/fish2020/oc44ch03.pdf; FAO Fisheries Department, *The State of World Fisheries and Aquaculture 2004,* part 1, *World Review of Fisheries and Aquaculture* (Rome: FAO, 2004), www.fao.org/docrep/007/y5600e/y5600e04.htm#p_1.

4. The Environmental Defense Fund was central to making this "market-mechanism" work for the halibut fishery.

5. The Clorox Company, "Clorox History," 2008, www.clorox.com/our_story/article.php?subsection=our_commitment&article_id=clorox_history.

6. The Clorox Company, "Clorox Annual Report 2005: Letter to the Shareholders," 2005, www.thecloroxcompany.com/investors/financialinfo/annreports/clxar05/Clorox_letter.pdf.

7. Bill Morrissey, phone interview with author, 3 July 2008.

8. Jessica Buttimer, phone interview with author, 3 July 2008.

9. Ashely Braun, "When a Bleach Company Cries Sustainable," *Sustainable Brands Weekly,* 2008, Sustainable Life Media, www.sustainablebrands08.com/sb08blog/when_a_bleach_company_cries_sustainable.

10. Reuters, "Wal-Mart Customers to Experience New Green Works Natural Cleaners from Clorox," *Thomson Reuters,* 14 January 2008, www.reuters.com/article/idUS136235+14-Jan-2008+PRN20080114.

11. Carl Pope, quoted in Sierra Club press release.

12. Ronald Bailey, "Dematerializing the Economy," *Reason Online,* 5 September 2008, www.reason.com/news/show/34879.html.

13. Jack Ewing, "Upwardly Mobile in Africa," *BusinessWeek,* 13 September 2007, http://www.businessweek.com/globalbiz/content/sep2007/gb20070913_705733.htm.

14. William Easterly, "A Modest Proposal, Review of 'The End of Poverty' by Jeffrey Sachs," *Washington Post,* 13 March 2005, www.washingtonpost.com/wp-dyn/articles/A25562-2005Mar10.html.

15. Ewing, "Upwardly Mobile in Africa."

16. http://thinkexist.com/quotation/whats_the_use_of_a_fine_house_if_you_haven-t_got/208880.html.

17. FAO, "Global Forest Resources Assessment 2005," Food and Agriculture Organization of the United Nations Forestry Paper 147, Rome, 2005.

18. Energy Information Administration official statistics for 2005.

19. Interview with author, 24 March 2009.

20. Boris Worm et al., "Impacts of Biodiversity Loss on Ocean Ecosystem Services," *Science,* 3 November 2006, 787.

21. Yuwei Zhang, "Climate Change: How It Impacts Us All," *UN Chronicle,* online edition, www.un.org/Pubs/chronicle/2007/webArticles/092107_dpi_ngo_climatechange.htm#.

22. Gregg Easterbrook, *The Progress Paradox: How Life Gets Better While People Feel Worse* (New York: Random House, 2004).

23. U.S. Census Bureau, "Housing Vacancies and Homeownership," www.census.gov/hhes/www/housing/hvs/annual05/ann05t12.html; U.S. Census Bureau, Census of Housing, "Historical Census of Housing Tables," www.census.gov/hhes/www/housing/census/historic/owner.html.

24. Elizabeth Arias, "United States Life Tables, 2004," *National Vital Statistics Reports* 56, no. 9 (December 2007) (Hyattsville, MD: CDC National Center for Health Statistics, 2007), www.cdc.gov/nchs/data/nvsr/nvsr56/nvsr56_09.pdf; Central Intelligence Agency, *CIA World Factbook 2008,* www.cia.gov/library/publications/the-world-factbook/rankorder/2102rank.html.

25. For African American incomes, see Gregg Easterbrook, *The Progress Paradox: How Life Gets Better While People Feel Worse* (New York: Random House, 2004). The median household income in South Africa is 74,589 rands (Statistics of South Africa, "Income and Expenditure of Households 2005/2006: Statistical Release," 4 March 2008, www.statssa.gov.za/publications/statskeyfindings.asp?PPN=P0100&SCH=4108), which is based on the current rand-to-dollar conversion ratio of 0.0989 as of December 2008 (XE, "Universal Currency Converter," www.xe.com/ucc/convert.cgi) and multiplied by the purchasing power parity (PPP) ratio (International Monetary Fund, "World Economic and Financial Surveys, World Economic Outlook Database," April 2007, www.imf.org/external/pubs/ft/weo/2007/01/data/index.aspx). For African income, see Patrick Honohan, "African Finance for the 21st Century," *International Monetary Fund,* Trinity College, Dublin, 5 March 2008, www.imf.org/external/np/seminars/eng/2008/afrfin/pdf/honohan.pdf.

26. Easterbrook, *The Progress Paradox,* 49; "Bahrain: Increase in Infant Mortality Rate," *Women Gateway,* 2008, www.womengateway.com/enwg/Life+Style/Health/healthnws1.htm.

27. Easterbrook, *The Progress Paradox.*

28. Whaples, "Hours of Work in U.S. History," EH.NET. 2008. Wake Forest University: http://eh.net/encyclopedia/article/whaples.work.hours.us; U.S. Department of Labor, Bureau of Labor Statistics, "Employment Situation Summary," January 2009, http://www.bls.gov/news.release/empsit.nr0.htm.

29. Easterbrook, *The Progress Paradox,* 11.

30. Theodore Caplow, Louis Hicks, and Ben J. Wattenberg, *The First Measured Century: An Illustrated Guide to Trends in America, 1900–2000* (Washington, DC: AEI Press, 2001), 8.

31. For the U.S. cancer rate, see Easterbrook, *The Progress Paradox,* 49; for Asia's rate, see Simeon Bennett and Kanoko Matsuyama, "Asia's Cancer Rate May More Than Double by 2020," *International Herald Tribune,* 23 April 2007, www.iht.com/articles/2007/04/23/news/cancer.php.

32. InflationData.com, "Historical Crude Oil Prices," 12 June 2008, www.inflationdata.com/inflation/Inflation_Rate/Historical_Oil_Prices_Table.asp.

33. Jeffrey Brown, "George W. Bush, Meet M. King Hubbert," 26 March 2008, http://graphoilogy.blogspot.com/2007/03/march-26-2007-by-jeffrey-j.html; M. King Hubbert, "Nuclear Energy and the Fossil Fuels," Shell Development

Company, Houston, 7 March 1956, www.hubbertpeak.com/Hubbert/1956/1956.pdf. Hubbert is also credited with this aphorism: "Our ignorance is not so vast as our failure to use what we know."

34. Richard C. Duncan, "The Peak of World Oil Production and the Road to the Olduvai Gorge," *Population & Environment* 22, no. 5 (November 2001): 503–522.

35. http://www.treehugger.com/files/2005/07/chevrontexaco_p.php.

36. Scott McCartney, "Flying Stinks Especially for the Airlines," *Wall Street Journal,* 10 June 2008, http://online.wsj.com/article/SB121304736426558641.html?mod=2_1367_topbox%3C/p%3E%3Cp%3E.

37. Chris Huntley, "Dow Responds to Surging Energy Costs," The Dow Chemical Company, Midland, MI, 28 May 2008, http://news.dow.com/dow_news/corporate/2008/20080528a.htm.

38. Andrew Liveris, quoted in Christopher Hinton, "Dow Chemical to Raise Product Prices by 20%," *Market Watch,* 28 May 2008, www.marketwatch.com/news/story/dow-chemical-ups-prices-ceo/story.aspx?guid={F34B0644-3E2E-4128-8035-ECC717FFB9F8}.

39. Joe Klein, "The Full Obama Interview," Swampland blog at Time.com, 12 October 2008, http://swampland.blogs.time.com/2008/10/23/the_full_obama_interview/.

40. U.S. Department of Energy, "Solar History Timeline: 1900s," Solar Energy Technologies Program, U.S. DOE, 11 July 2008, www1.eere.energy.gov/solar/solar_time_1900.html; John Perlin, "Solar Cells from Space to Earth," *Miller-McCune,* 25 March 2008, www.miller-mccune.com/article/solar-cells-from-space-to-earth.

41. Publicis is the holding company that owns Saatchi & Saatchi.

42. Ray Kurzweil and Chris Meyer, "Understanding the Accelerating Rate of Change," *Perspectives on Business Innovation,* 1 May 2003, available at www.kurzweilai.net/articles/art0563.html?printable=1.

Chapter Three

1. Saatchi & Saatchi X, the shopper marketing arm of Saatchi & Saatchi, uses ShopperFocus, a panel of 1,200 average American shoppers whom they query regularly to find insights on shopping. According to X research, the average American shopper shops at five stores to complete his or her basic shopping missions. You can learn more about Saatchi X at www.saatchix.com.

2. U.S. Bureau of Labor Statistics, "Economic News Release," 2007, table 3, http://www.bls.gov/news.release/atus.t08.htm.

3. At the incidental mention of Lay's potato chips, I should mention that we provide consulting services to Frito-Lay. We helped them communicate their launch of a new solar power initiative for Sun-Chips, and we continue to support them in engaging their employees with the Personal Sustainability Project.

4. By *value brands,* I'm referring to a brand that is viewed as having a high performance-to-cost ratio. In other words, it's not cheap (or lacking in quality), but it's not a luxury item, either.

5. Jacob Gordon, "The TH Interview: Andy Ruben & Matt Kissler of Walmart," *Treehugger Radio,* 7 November 2007, www.treehugger.com/files/2007/11/the_th_interview_andy_and_matt.php.

6. Accessed and priced at $740 after online discounts at a leading "sustainable living" online store Gaia, Inc., www.gaiam.com/product/eco-home-outdoor/bedroom/sheets-bedding/lucia+fitted+sheet.do. Here's the full description: "Steeped in the hues of an ocean sunset, our Lucia jacquard bedding infuses your bedroom with Mediterranean flair. Our mill in Portugal, known for it's [sic] luxury bedding, weaves 100 percent organic cotton into a 300 thread count sateen fabric, free of harsh chemical softeners or chlorine. Duvet and shams are designed with a reversing contrast jacquard. Solid sheets and pillowcases feature a solid color with contrasting hem. Low eco-impact dyes."

7. Ellen Wulfhorst, "Many US workers live paycheck to paycheck-survey," Reuters, 12 March 2007, www.boston.com/jobs/news/articles/2007/03/12/many_us_workers_live_paycheck_to_paycheck_survey/.

8. This insight comes from an interview with Andy Murray, Worldwide CEO of Saatchi & Saatchi X.

9. An exception to this is when shoppers participate in the U.S. WIC (Women, Infants and Children) program, in which the federal government subsidizes the purchase of high-protein, healthy foods. These shoppers use their WIC checks to buy milk, eggs, and cheese. There's also a wonderful, yet small, program called the Farmer's Market Nutrition Program, which subsidizes the purchase of fruits and vegetables in forty-six states in the United States.

10. Daniel Franklin, "The World in 2009: The Year of Unsustainability," *Economist,* 19 November 2008, www.economist.com/theworldin/Printer-Friendly.cfm?story_id=12494427.

11. Johnson & Johnson, "Our Credo," Johnson & Johnson Web page, www.jnj.com/wps/wcm/connect/30e290804ae70eb4bc4afc0f0a50cff8/our-credo.pdf?MOD=AJPERES. We have provided sustainability consulting services to Johnson & Johnson.

12. J.C.Penney Company, Inc., "Our Culture," 2008, www.jcpenney.net/careers/N3_our_culture/default.aspx.

13. Hilton, "Hilton Hotels Corporation Announces Sustainability Goals," press release, 4 June 2008, www.hiltongardeninnfranchise.com/marketing/sustainability.asp.

14. Procter & Gamble, "P&G 2007 Sustainability Report, Executive Summary," 2007, www.pg.com/company/our_commitment/pdfs/gsr07_execsum.pdf. We have provided sustainability consulting services to P&G and P&G is Saatchi & Saatchi's (our parent company's) largest single client.

15. This information is from Amory Lovins, who has spent the last decade giving me tidbits like this. Amory, like me, was one of the people mentored by David Brower. Amory Lovins, "Profitable, Business Driven Solutions to the Climate, Oil & Nuclear Proliferation Problems," Rocky Mountain Institute, 23 February 2008, www.rmi.org/images/PDFs/Energy/BerlinVideo23ii08.pdf.

16. The term *cradle to cradle* refers to producing waste-free goods by recycling materials into new or similar products at the end of a product's intended life. For more information, see Product Life Institute, Geneva, Web page, www.product-life.org; Walter Stahel, *The Performance Economy* (Basingstoke: Palgrave Macmillan, 2006).

17. Interface Inc., "Progress Toward Zero: Ascending to Reach Sustainability," 2008, www.interfaceglobal.com/Sustainability/Progress-to-Zero.aspx.

18. Kevin Roberts has been a key advocate for sustainability in the Saatchi & Saatchi organization and among its clients. Cultural sustainability is of particular interest to him, as he lives in New Zealand, and preserving Maori culture is important to him.

19. Kevin Roberts, interview with the author, July 2008.

20. The General Mills subsidary Cascadian Farm does manufacture a product called Purely O's, which is basically organic Cheerios.

21. Procter & Gamble, "Tide Coldwater," 2007, www.tide.com/en_US/tidecoldwater/index.jsp.

22. Len Sauers, interview with the author, 7 August 2008.

23. P&G is a core client for Saatchi & Saatchi. I have worked with P&G on a number of insight projects, including one project on marketing strategy for Tide.

24. Marc Gunther, "Stonyfield Stirs Up the Yogurt Market," *Fortune,* 4 January 2008, http://money.cnn.com/2008/01/03/news/companies/gunther_yogurt.fortune/index.htm.

25. Gary Hirshberg, interview with the author, August 2008.

26. UPS employed software to make its routing more efficient for its ninety-five thousand trucks. One of its strategies was to have the trucks take fewer left turns. According to the *New York Times,* in one year, the effort shaved "28.5 million miles off [UPS] delivery routes, which has resulted in savings of roughly three million gallons of gas and . . . reduced CO_2 emissions by 31,000 metric tons." Joel Lovell, "Left-Hand-Turn Elimination," *New York Times,* 9 December 2007, www.nytimes.com/2007/12/09/magazine/09left-handturn.html.

27. Matthew Wheeland, "Selling Small, Thinking Big: P&G's Sustainable Innovations," Greenbiz.com, 10 July 2008, www.greenbiz.com/podcast/2008/07/10/selling-small-thinking-big.

28. Walmart Press Release. "Wal-Mart Concentrated Liquid Laundry Detergent," Walmart.com, May 2008, walmartstores.com/download/2328.pdf.

Chapter Four

1. Louis D. Brandeis, "Other People's Money—and How the Bankers Use It," *Harper's Weekly,* 1914. An entire copy of this work is available at http://library.louisville.edu/law/brandeis/opm-toc.html.

2. The public always seems to favor a laggard who finally owns up to his or her legacy and sets some audacious goals over a leader who commits to lead more. The clients I work with who have been striving for sustainability for a decade are always amazed when a competitor who is just beginning the journey gets accolades. It's like a ten-year-old child who takes his or her first step and gets applauded with no one asking why it took the kid so long to walk. I ascribe this to a little bit of affirmative action for those late to the game. Be assured, the leader who has always led is a safe bet for who will lead into the future.

3. Julie Schmit, "USDA Will Step Up Inspections at Slaughterhouse," *USA Today,* 18 February 2008, www.usatoday.com/money/industries/food/2008-02-18-meat-recall_N.htm.

4. Bob Krauter, "Felony Charges Filed in Westland Meat Packing Case," *Capital Press,* 15 February 2008. www.capitalpress.info/main.asp? SectionID=94&SubSectionID=801&ArticleID=39367&TM=14294.3.

5. The Super Sandwich Bale recycling program at Walmart allowed store associates to recycle fourteen types of materials in its normal baler. The program was developed by Walmart, Rocky Mountain Recycling, and BluSkye. Elanie Jarvik, "Super Sandwich Bale: Utah Man's Idea Nets Wholesale Recycling," *Deseret News,* 22 April 2008, www.deseretnews.com/article/content/mobile/1,5620,695272741,00.html?printView=true.

6. Don Richman, "Donald Valencia, 1952–2007: Starbucks Executive Left Corporate Career for Social Activism," *Seattle Post Intelligence,* 14 December 2008, http://seattlepi.nwsource.com/business/343600_obitvalencia15.html.

7. Simon Winchester, *The Professor and the Madman: A Tale of Murder, Insanity, and the Making of the Oxford English Dictionary* (New York: Harper Perennial, 1998).

8. Casey Harrell, Toxics Campaigner for Greenpeace International, e-mail conversation with author, 8 December 2008.

9. Linda Birnbaum and Daniele Staskal, "Brominated Flame Retardants: Cause for Concern?" *Environmental Health Perspectives* 112, no. 1 (January 2004) 9–17, www.ehponline.org/members/2003/6559/6559.html.

10. Greenpeace, "Green My Apple, Steve," Greenpeace campaign Web site, 26 September 2006, www.greenpeace.org/international/news/green-my-apple-260906; and Rick Hind, Legislative Director of Greenpeace's Toxics Campaign, e-mail correspondence with author, 5 December 2008. For more information, see Greenpeace, "Breaking News: Steve Jobs Announces Change in Policy," 2007,www.greenmyapple.org/. Full disclosure, I'm a long-time supporter of Greenpeace, and was twice elected to their International Board of Directors.

11. A Creative Commons license is a copyright issued by an eponymous non-profit organization that allows holders to grant a certain amount of rights to the public. See Creative Commons Web page, www.creativecommons.org.

12. YouTube, "Steve Jobs 2007 Keynote (Spoof Video)," 2008, www.youtube.com/watch?v=2Uo_4kyrkDc.

13. Steve Jobs, "A Greener Apple," 2008, www.apple.com/hotnews/agreener-apple/.

14. In the interest of full disclosure, I note here that I've written this book on a MacBook, although my next computer will be a Dell. Jason Reed, our IT director at Saatchi & Saatchi S, noticed how many boxes and how much extraneous packing material we were receiving when we bulk-ordered computers from Dell. He sent me some photos and ideas about ways to enhance its packaging. I sent his ideas to our technical consulting team in Boulder, and the information eventually ended up in the hands of Tod Arbogast, the director of sustainable business for Dell. Arbogast hired us to dive deeper into the recommendations, and Dell recently announced that it would cut 20 million pounds of packaging and save $8.1 million over four years. But just to give this some context, I asked Casey Harrell from Greenpeace what he thought about what Dell was doing. "Dell is slipping in our ranking, because there is a huge difference between the lovely words of Michael Dell and the company's actions on the ground (we are hearing rumblings that they are going to slide on their commitment to PVC/BFR [polyvinyl chloride and brominated flame retardant] phase-out)," he said. Suffice it to say that the entire technology industry still has a long way to go.

15. Carl Pope, chairman, Sierra Club, phone interview with author, July 2008.

16. Michael Shellenberger, president, Breakthrough Institute, interview with author, San Francisco, July 2008.

17. S. Greenhouse, "Apparel Industry Group Moves to End Sweatshops," *New York Times,* 9 April 1997, http://query.nytimes.com/gst/fullpage.html?res=9507E4DE143CF93AA35757C0A961958260&scp=2&sq=Nike percent2C+sweatshops&st=nyt.

18. P. Drier and R. Applebaum, "Campus Breakthrough on Sweatshop Labor, *Nation,* 1 June 2006.

19. S. Holmes and A. Bernstein, "The New Nike," *Business Week,* 20 September 2004, www.businessweek.com/magazine/content/04_38/b3900001_mz001.htm.

20. Lorrie Vogel, general manager, Considered Products, Nike, phone interview with author, 25 July 2008.

21. Amy Cortese, "Friend of Nature? Let's See Those Shoes," *New York Times,* 7 March 2007.

22. Betsy Blaisdell, manager, environmental stewardship, Timberland, phone interview with author, 23 July 2008.

23. http://www.businesswire.com/portal/site/google/?ndmViewId=news_view&newsId=20090205005371&newsLang=en.

24. Jeffrey Swartz, quoted in "The Green: Interview, Eco-BizEcoBiz:—Timberland," *EcoBiz,* online program, The Sundance Channel, 2008, www.sundancechannel.com/videos/2302044000nline Video. Youtube. http://www.youtube.com/watch?v=JTbJULvD6LY.

25. John Elkington, telephone and e-mail interview with the author, 30 June 2008.

26. Global Reporting Initiative, "Sustainability Reporting Guidelines," 2006, www.globalreporting.org/NR/rdonlyres/ED9E9B36-AB54-4DE1-BFF2-5F735235CA44/0/G3_GuidelinesENU.pdf.

27. G.S. Sustaina, *Expanding and Enhancing,* 30 June 2008.

28. Ibid., 52.

29. William Baue, "A Brief History of Sustainability Reporting," Social Funds Web site, 2 July 2004, www.socialfunds.com/news/article.cgi/1459.html.

30. Nongovernmental organizations like CERES and the As You Sow foundation, alongside socially conscious investors like Trillium Asset Management and Calvert, have led the charge to demand sustainability reports in *Fortune* 500 companies.

31. We have provided consulting services to General Electric.

32. This is a training example I learned from the people at Duke Energy, which has built a safety culture over the last decade.

33. DuPont, "DuPont Expands Sustainability Commitments to Include R&D, Revenue Goals," press release, 10 October 2006, http://vocuspr.vocus.com/VocusPR30/Newsroom/Query.aspx?SiteName=DupontNew&Entity=PRAsset&SF_PRAsset_PRAssetID_EQ=103458&XSL=Press Release&Cache=False.

34. DuPont, "2007 DuPont Excellence Awards, Sustainable Growth," company brochure, 2007, available at www2.dupont.com/Sustainability/en_US/assets/downloads/2007_SG_award_brochure.pdf.

35. Compensation Resources, Inc., "Comp Committees Link Incentive Pay Environmental Goals," 2008, www.compensationresources.com/pressroom/comp-committees-link-incentive-pay-environmental-goals.php. We have provided employee engagement consulting services to Duke Energy.

Chapter Five

1. "Northwest Highlights," *Northwest Science & Technology* (winter 2006), https://depts.washington.edu/nwst/issues/index.php?issueID=winter_2006&storyID=781.

2. ConAgra, "ConAgra Foods Announces Test Finds Salmonella in Its Peanut Butter," press release, 22 February 2007, http://investor.conagrafoods.com/phoenix.zhtml?c=97518&p=irol-newsArticlemedia&ID=966490&highlight.

3. Michael Moss, "Peanut Case Shows Holes in Safety Net," 8 February, 2009, http://www.nytimes.com/2009/02/09/us/09peanuts.html?ref=us.

4. Arnold Bakker and William Schaufeli, "Positive Organizational Behavior: Engaged Employees in Flourishing Organizations," *Journal of Organizational Behavior* 29, no. 2 (15 January 2008): 147–154, describe engagement as "a set of motivating resources such as support and recognition from colleagues and supervisors, performance feedback, opportunities for learning and development, and opportunities for skill use."

5. Steve Crabtree, "Engagement Keeps the Doctor Away," *Gallup Management Journal,* 13 January 2005, http://gmj.gallup.com/content/14500/Engagement-Keeps-Doctor-Away.aspx.

6. "Employee Engagement: A Review of Current Research and Its Implications," research report E-0010-06-RR, The Conference Board, New York, 11 September 2006, www.conference-board.org/knowledge/knowledgeProd.cfm?id=1238&nav=hr.

7. Katharine Esty and Mindy Gewirtz, "Creating a Culture of Employee Engagement," *Boston.com,* 23 July 2008, www.boston.com/jobs/nehra/062308.shtml.

8. Background on the Gallup Survey of Employee Development, also called the Q12, can be found at Gallup, Inc., "Gallup Study: Engaged Employees Inspire Company Innovation," *Gallup Management Journal,* 12 October 2006, http://gmj.gallup.com/content/24880/Gallup-Study-Engaged-Employees-Inspire-Company.aspx.

9. Edge Foundation, "Eudaemonia, The Good Life: A Talk with Martin Seligman," *Edge* 135 (23 March 2004), http://edge.org/3rd_culture/seligman04/seligman_index.html.

10. For resources on positive psychology, see, Martin Seligman, *Authentic Happiness: Using the New Positive Psychology to Realize Your Potential for Lasting Fulfillment* (New York: Free Press, 2004); and Chris Peterson, *A Primer in Positive Psychology* (New York: Oxford University Press, 2006).

11. S. Lyubomirsky, L. King, and E. Diener, "The Benefits of Frequent Positive Affect: Does Happiness Lead to Success?" *Psychological Bulletin* 131 (2005): 803–855.

12. Venkatesh Shankar et al., "Assessing Innovation Metrics: McKinsey Global Survey Result," *McKinsey Quarterly,* November 2008, www.mckinseyquarterly.com/Strategy/Innovation/McKinsey_Global_Survey_Results_Assessing_innovation_metrics_2243?pagenum=3.

13. Michael Barbaro from the *New York Times* was the first reporter to break the story that I was working with Walmart. I had mistakenly tried to keep it quiet so that we could focus on the work and not on telling the story. That's a good example of how transparency would have been a better policy. Much of the story of the launch of the Personal Sustainability Project

was told in Danielle Sacks, "Working with the Enemy," *Fast Company,* September 2007. I've taken strides to use Barbaro's and Sacks's reporting and other public sources to describe what's going in Walmart in terms of sustainability. The full story of how Walmart turned itself around and became one of the top global sustainability leaders is extraordinary and does need to be told.

14. PSP, Personal Sustainability, and the Personal Sustainability Project are all registered trademarks of Saatchi & Saatchi S. Why? Our vision is to develop the framework, enhance its quality, attract a billion people to join, and then put PSP into the public trust.

15. I told Ruth and Amanda's story in my speech, "The Birth of Blue," Commonwealth Club, 10 April 2008. The text of that speech can be found at: gristmill. grist.org/story/2008/4/11/153519/830.

16. City-Data.com, "Vancouver, Washington," Onboard Informatics, 2008, www.city-data.com/city/Vancouver-Washington.html.

17. Wilmar B. Schaufeli, Arnold B. Bakker, and Marisa Salanova, "The Measurement of Work Engagement with a Short Questionnaire," *Educational and Psychological Measurement* 66, no. 4 (2006): 701–716, http://epm.sagepub. com/cgi/content/abstract/66/4/701.

18. The Climate Group, Members Web page, 2008, www.theclimategroup.org/ about/members_and_partners/members/bskyb. September 2008, www.reuters. com/article/pressRelease/idUS130782+24-Sep-2008+PRN20080924.

19. Joan Kennedy, president, HMC, and senior vice president, WellPoint Inc., phone interview with the author, 22 August 2008.

20. Brod Perkins, e-mail to author, February 9, 2009.

Chapter Six

1. Death Valley National Park was protected (along with the Mojave National Preserve and Joshua Tree National Park) through the California Desert Protection Act, passed by the U.S. Congress in 1994. I was lucky to have worked closely with Elden Hughes, Judy Anderson, and Jim Dodson on this campaign—the last national park victory in the United States.

2. What is selling out? Selling out describes when someone trades his or her reputation or values for monetary gain. When I first started consulting with Walmart, I was begged by friends and supporters not to accept its money. One generous foundation even offered to pay me so that I wouldn't bear the insult of a check from Walmart. But since my North Star has been to build a world full of happy people living on a healthy planet, my choice was clear. Working with the largest company on the planet, in an effort that seemed both prudent and well intentioned, would be a way to move my values forward. It's better to take a risk and fail than to be arrogant and useless.

3. Environmental News Service, "Greenpeace Links McDonald's with Amazon Destruction," 6 April 2006, www.ens-newswire.com/ens/apr2006/2006-04-06-01.asp.

4. Greenpeace, "Eating Up the Amazon," 6 April 2006, www.greenpeace.org/international/press/reports/eating-up-the-amazon/.

5. World Wildlife Foundation, "Reducing Deforestation Is Key to Addressing Climate Change, WWF Official Tells Congress," press release, 22 April 2008, www.worldwildlife.org/who/media/press/2008/WWFPresitem 8733.html.

6. Greenpeace, "Deforestation and Climate Change," 2008, www.greenpeace.org.uk/forests/climate-change.

7. EarthTrends, "Brazil," World Resources Institute, 2007, http://earthtrends.wri.org/povlinks/country/brazil.php.

8. Marcelo Furtado, executive director, Greenpeace Brazil, interview and meetings, Sao Paolo, Brazil, 10 September 2007.

9. BBC, "Arrests at Fast Food Store Demo," 6 April 2006, http://news.bbc.co.uk/2/hi/uk_news/england/manchester/4882444.stm.

10. Bob Langert, interview with the author, 30 July 2008.

11. Marc Kaufman, "New Allies on the Amazon," *Washington Post,* 24 April 2007, www.washingtonpost.com/wp-dyn/content/article/2007/04/23/AR2007042301903.html.

12. Bob Langert, vice president, corporate social responsibility, McDonald's, phone interview with author, August 2008.

13. Kaufman, "New Allies on the Amazon."

14. Walmart, "About Us," http://walmartstores.com/AboutUs/.

15. Full disclaimer: In December 2008, Saatchi & Saatchi S advised Dell on the development of its packaging strategy. See Dell, "Dell Expands Global Green-Packaging Strategy to Drive Cost and Environmental Savings," 16 December 2008, www.dell.com/content/topics/global.aspx/corp/pressoffice/en/2008/2008_12_16_rr_000?c=us&l=en&s=corp.

16. Waste News, "Dell Inc. Announces Computer Take-Back Program," 19 December 2008, www.cambriarecycles.org/Recycle/DellComputerTakeback.htm. For more information on Dell's recycling program, see Dell, "Dell Product Recycling," http://support.dell.com/support/topics/global.aspx/support/recycling/en/product_recycle?c=us&l=en&s=gen.

17. Tod Arbogast, director of sustainable business, phone interview with author, 11 July 2008.

18. Marc Gunther, "Dell Gets on the Environmental Bandwagon," *Fortune,* 8 March 2007, http://money.cnn.com/2007/03/08/magazines/fortune/pluggedin_gunther_dellrecycle.fortune/index.htm.

19. The Cristina Foundation is a nonprofit organization that matches donated computer equipment with needy schools and nonprofit organizations around the world (see www.cristina.org).

20. Ben Ames, "Dell Pushes Texas e-Cycling Law," *Washington Post,* 11 June 2007, www.washingtonpost.com/wp-dyn/content/article/2007/06/11/AR2007061100033.html.

Chapter Seven

1. I covered this story earlier in my speech, "The Birth of Blue," Commonwealth Club, San Francisco, 10 April 2008. The speech can be found at: gristmill.grist.org/story/2008/4/11/153519/830.

2. National Center for Chronic Disease Prevention and Health Promotion, "Diabetes: Disabling Disease to Double by 2050," 17 September 2008, Centers for Disease Control and Prevention, www.cdc.gov/nccdphp/publications/aag/ddt.htm.

3. The statistics presented here are actually those pulled from the end of seven months of project deployment in the United States only and are based on associates' reporting. The actual numbers to date are most likely significantly higher. They have been presented previously in Wal-Mart's first sustainability report.

4. Xerox, "Report on Global Citizenship," 2007, www.xerox.com/downloads/usa/en/x/Xerox_Global_Citizenship_Report_2007.pdf.

5. Patrica Calkins, vice president of environment, health, and safety, phone interview with author, 11 December 2008.

6. Adam Lowry, cofounder and chief greenskeeper, method, phone interview with author, 10 July 2008.

7. The Iroquois constitution is one of the most compelling documents you'll ever read. See National Public Telecomputing Network; Gerald Murphy, preparer; and Glenn Welker, compiler; "The Constitution of the Iroquois Nations: The Great Binding Law—*Gayanashagowa*," Indigenous Peoples Literature Web page, www.indigenouspeople.net/iroqcon.htm.

8. Jeffrey Hollender, CEO, Seventh Generation, phone interview with author, August 2008.

9. Hannah Hoag, "The Missing Greenhouse Gas," *Nature,* 10 July 2008, www.nature.com/climate/2008/0808/full/climate.2008.72.html.

10. Jim Thomas, vice president, CSR, JCPenney, conversation with author, Plano, TX, 11 July 2008.

11. One of the seminal works that imprinted the concept of ecological limits to the American public (and the green movement in the United States) was Donella H. Meadows, Dennis L. Meadows, Jørgen Randers, and William W. Behrens III, *Limits to Growth* (New York: Universe Books, 1972). Donella Meadows followed up the book with the suggestion of twelve leverage points that were a systemic response to globalization, a process epitomized by the North American Free Trade Agreement. While the limits aren't in question, a blue framework proposes that orienting a movement around limits instead

of opportunities tends to bring out the worst in humanity instead of the best. Efforts toward population control, for example, which exemplify the greatest "antihuman" wing of the green movement, were born out of this same limits context.

12. In 2002, I was asked by the Center for Urban Education About Sustainable Agriculture (CUESA), in San Francisco, to consult on its business plan for building a robust permanent farmers market in the historic Ferry Building in San Francisco. At the time, there was an internal battle in the organization between those who wanted to be organic and those who wanted to be sustainable. *Organic* is a technical certification that the U.S. Department of Agriculture defines as "raised without using most conventional pesticides, petroleum-based fertilizers, or sewage sludge-based fertilizers." *Sustainable* is much harder to define but requires that you could continue producing the crop forever without diminishing the social, economic, environmental, and cultural resources you require to produce that crop. I was quickly won over by the advocates for sustainable farming, as they were much more concerned with social issues like price and availability than in the marketing benefit that using the word *organic* presented. The Bay Area has continued to produce thought leadership in the area. Berkeley author Michael Pollan is perhaps the best chronicler of our modern food woes, and Berkeley chef Alice Waters is one of the best sustainable chefs in the world. If you're in San Francisco, make sure you stop by the Ferry Plaza to see the market.

Conclusion

1. For a compelling presentation of this fact, go to www.192021.com.

2. http://news.bbc.co.uk/2/hi/health/4334651.stm

3. World Health Organization, "Obesity and Overweight" fact sheet, September 2006, http:// www.who.int/mediacentre/factsheets/fs3111/en/index.html.

4. Adlai Stevenson, speech to the UN Economic and Social Council, Geneva, Switzerland, 9 July 1965.

5. Gannon Jones, vice president of marketing, Frito-Lay, e-mail interview with author, 23 July 2008.

6. *Expanding and Enhancing,* GS Sustain research report, 30 June 2008, 1.

7. Kevin Roberts, global CEO of Saatchi & Saatchi, interview and meetings with the author, San Francisco, 2 October 2008.

8. http://articles.latimes.com/2007/sep/19/local/me-traffic19; http://www.treehugger.com/files/2007/09/wasting_away_in.php.

9. http://www.cbc.ca/world/story/2008/05/08/f-natural-disasters-history.html.

10. As quoted by Richard Dawkins in his 2001 eulogy for Adams.

Index

About the Author

ADAM WERBACH is widely known as one of the foremost experts in sustainability strategy. In 1996, at age twenty-three, Werbach was elected the youngest-ever President of the Sierra Club, the oldest and largest environmental organization in the United States. Since then, Werbach has travelled the world championing sustainability, built and sold three companies, and merged with global ideas company Saatchi & Saatchi to create the world's largest sustainability agency, Saatchi & Saatchi S.

As Global CEO of Saatchi & Saatchi S, Werbach guides sustainability work from China to South Africa to Brazil, advising companies with nearly $1 trillion in combined annual sales, including Walmart, Procter & Gamble, General Mills, and NBC Universal. Werbach worked with Walmart to engage the company's 1.9 million associates in its sustainability effort, creating the Personal Sustainability Project ("PSP").

Twice elected to the International Board of Greenpeace, Werbach is a frequent commentator on sustainable business, appearing on networks including BBC, NPR, and CNN, and shows ranging from the *The O'Reilly Factor* to *Charlie Rose*. He lives in San Francisco's Bernal Heights with his wife Lyn and children Mila, Pearl, and Simon.

To contact Adam e-mail him at awerbach@saatchis.com or find him on Facebook. Go to www.strategyforsustainability.com for additional chapters, tools, and resources on *Strategy for Sustainability,* and to register for updates.

SMALL STEPS MATTER

Picking up *Strategy for Sustainability* was the first step in a journey toward sustainability for you and your business.

But it doesn't end here.

Join Adam Werbach at **www.strategyforsustainability.com** to learn more about how to put these ideas into action.

Visit the site to:

- Find the best strategy to address your company's unique challenges
- Identify gaps in your sustainability plans and access resources to get you up to speed
- Develop your own personal sustainability practice

It's time to take another small step.

VISIT THE WEB SITE TODAY:
www.strategyforsustainability.com